NO TURNING BACK

"Most of us have been in a position of sacrificing to win the applause of others more than resting in God's acceptance. In *No Turning Back*, Rashawn takes us on his spiritual journey of discovering how to turn self-seeking love into an awareness of God's love. Jesus is the path and the prize, and the walk of faith is often a winding road. Instead of looking back, we should look forward to what is ahead: eternal life with Jesus."

Candace Cameron Bure, actress, producer, and *New York Times* bestselling author

"With a palpable authenticity, Rashawn writes a heartfelt and uplifting book, unpacking the truth of God's Word for the discouraged and doubtful. *No Turning Back* will inspire, equip, and encourage you to follow Jesus through the storms, resting in His promises as He transforms us into who He has called us to be."

Benjamin Watson, NFL Super Bowl champion, author of *Under Our Skin*, speaker, and commentator

"Rashawn Copeland lives 100 percent totally all-in for Jesus, and because of that his life is a wild, joyous, difference-making adventure 24/7! In his inspiring book *No Turning Back*, Rashawn gives us a practical guide for how we can live that kind of life. This book is a must-read for all who want to keep our focus on Jesus and never turn back!"

Dave Ferguson, lead visionary of NewThing and author of *B.L.E.S.S.: 5 Everyday Ways to Love Your Neighbor and Change the World*

"*No Turning Back* will keep you turning pages of encouragement and engaging stories that push you deeper into your relationship with Jesus. Rashawn instantly became someone I love to be around! I was thrilled to see his sincerity, his authenticity, and the joy he's found in Jesus come out in this book. You're going to really enjoy the journey ahead."

Jonathan "JP" Pokluda, bestselling author, voice of *The Becoming Something* podcast, and pastor of Harris Creek

"Not long ago my thirteen-year-old son and I read through Rashawn's first book, *Start Where You Are*, together. It was so good! The only thing we didn't like about it was that it came to an end. But now we have another book to dive into together. The longer I live, the more I want to finish the Christian race well and hear the words, 'Well done, good and faithful servant." *No Turning Back* offers practical and personal encouragement to faithfully live the Christian life, teaching us to daily stay on the path and focus on the prize: Jesus. Whether you are thirteen, forty-seven, or one hundred and seven, Rashawn helps you keep your eyes on the prize! Amid life's hardships, struggles, and even death, his words will refresh your soul and spur you on to finish well. And perhaps, like me, you'll find that Rashawn is the man you want speaking into your teenagers' lives as well."

Wendy Speake, author of *The 40-Day Sugar Fast*
and *The 40-Day Social Media Fast*

"In the last year Rashawn has become a great friend, supporter, and, more importantly, brother in the Lord to me. You will surely be inspired and encouraged by this book to never settle, to find a way to rejoice even through trial, and to allow the trials of life to refine your character instead of destroy it."

Remi Adeleke, former Navy Seal, author
of the bestselling *Transformed*, and actor
in *Transformers: The Last Knight*

"Jesus warned of a time when 'Sin will be rampant everywhere, and the love of many will grow cold.' Then he added, 'But the one who endures to the end will be saved' (Matt. 24:12–13). Well, think of Rashawn Copeland's book *No Turning Back* as endurance lessons from a compassionate fellow traveler whose seasoned advice can help you grow and persevere in your faith. Apply his biblical insights and you can increasingly become, like Rashawn, a spiritual inspiration to the people all around you!"

Mark Mittelberg, executive director of the Lee Strobel Center
for Evangelism and Applied Apologetics at Colorado Christian
University, and author of the book and course *Contagious Faith*

"My dear friend Rashawn Copeland has done it again! *No Turning Back* will inspire, equip, and challenge you to know Jesus and to make Jesus known. This book is both winsome and transparent. Everyone goes through seasons of doubt and discouragement, and this book will help you realize you are not alone. So get a copy for yourself and one for a friend who needs this kind of hope. Read it together. Journey together. Be uplifted together."

Shane Pruitt, national next gen director of North
American Mission Board (NAMB) and author
of *9 Common Lies Christians Believe*

NO TURNING BACK

ESCAPE YOUR PAST, EMPOWER YOUR PRESENT,
AND EXPERIENCE GOD'S BEST FOR YOU

RASHAWN COPELAND

BakerBooks

a division of Baker Publishing Group
Grand Rapids, Michigan

© 2022 by Rashawn Copeland

Published by Baker Books
a division of Baker Publishing Group
PO Box 6287, Grand Rapids, MI 49516-6287
www.bakerbooks.com

Printed in the United States of America

Library of Congress Cataloging-in-Publication Data
Names: Copeland, Rashawn, 1987– author.
Title: No turning back : escape your past, empower your present, and experience God's best for you / Rashawn Copeland.
Description: Grand Rapids, MI : Baker Books, a division of Baker Publishing Group, [2022] | Includes bibliographical references.
Identifiers: LCCN 2021030424 | ISBN 9781540900128 | ISBN 9781540902061 (casebound) | ISBN 9781493434077 (ebook)
Subjects: LCSH: Self-actualization (Psychology)—Religious aspects—Christianity. | Spiritual formation.
Classification: LCC BV4598.2 .C665 2022 | DDC 204/.4—dc23
LC record available at https://lccn.loc.gov/2021030424

The author is represented by MacGregor & Luedeke Literary.

Some names and details have been changed to protect the privacy of the individuals involved.

22   23   24   25   26   27   28   7   6   5   4   3   2   1

To my fourteen-year-old spiritual sister,
Berklee Maguire,
who lost her life in a devastating
propane tank blast in 2020.
Oh, sweet sister, you are beloved.
You inspired these words,
and your life serves as a reminder
to us all to live in His joy and never turn back.
#LiveLikeBerk

CONTENTS

Foreword by Carlos Whittaker   11
Forethought   13
Introduction: The Journey   15

1   From Forgetting Who You Were to Remembering Who You Are   23

2   From Dirty Desires to Desiring God   41

3   From Toxic Thinking to Transformative Truth   59

4   From Your Plan to God's Purpose   77

5   From Being Spilled Empty to Being Filled with Plenty   95

6   From Self-Reliance to Relying on God's Power   113

7   From Slavery to Kinship   131

8   From Dying Religion to Living Relationship   151

9   From Risk-Free Living to Radical Faith   171

Afterthought: Your Battle Cry—No Turning Back!   195
Acknowledgments   205
Notes   209

Foreword

WHEN MY LIFE FELL APART in 2011, I was faced with a decision: to chase after healing or chase after feeling. You see, my feelings were all over the place. I felt abandoned by God. I felt I could just continue to medicate my pain. I felt the work required to get my life back on track was just too much.

To medicate the pain is the easy road. But it is the empty road. My road to recovery was filled with good intentions but poor decisions.

I honestly wish *No Turning Back* had been available for my journey back then. This incredible book by my good friend Rashawn invites you to rediscover the joy that's found in finishing your race strong in Jesus, with Jesus, and like Jesus. Rashawn has cracked the code on how exactly to move from discouragement and disappointment to healing. His story lays out for us a road map to healing in a way that few others could have done.

I pray that this book does for you what it did for me. Now I feel prepared to allow my future disappointments to direct me to the destination of restoration.

Your healing is closer than you think. And Rashawn's words will take you there.

Inside this book you'll find joy in the jabs of disappointment, peace in the sting of discouragement, biblical wisdom, and practical advice. I can't think of a better author for this topic. Rashawn's joyful personality shines brightly through the pages. As a result, you'll see why I consider him a model of Christian hope and healing.

Carlos Whittaker, bestselling author
of *Kill the Spider* and *Enter Wild*

Forethought

WHEN JESUS WAS TALKING to Peter and the crowd, He began to tell them about what they must do to be His disciples and the suffering they must endure. Ouch! People walked away. They just left! When Jesus talked about eating His own body and drinking His blood (see John 6:53–60), people deserted. It didn't make sense to them. And then Jesus asked His disciples, "You do not want to leave too, do you?" (v. 67 NIV). Peter answered with something so profound. He said, "Lord, to whom shall we go? You have the words of eternal life" (v. 68).

When life gets dark and suffering becomes unbearable—when things don't make sense—where are you going to go? What are you going to turn to? Hedonism? Materialism? Video games? Alcohol? Drugs? Sex? These things may provide some type of immediate relief; however, in the long-term they will leave you bitter, angry, and alone. Again and again, without wavering, we must choose the light. No matter how dark the persecution or how sweet the pleasures of this fleeting world seem, the greatest place to be is steady on the path and focused on the prize.

Introduction

THE JOURNEY

IS THIS ALL THERE IS?

I just thought I'd feel different.

Will things ever change?

Thoughts raced through my mind. Thursday morning approached, and I wondered what reason I could give my pastor for canceling our weekly discipleship meeting . . . again. We had been studying the book of John, and it was definitely fascinating, but I just didn't feel like I measured up to what I was reading nor to the other Christians around me. Pastor Sam and I had been meeting for four months, and I couldn't bring myself to admit that I wasn't getting anywhere. I felt discouraged . . . defeated . . . doubtful.

And it definitely wasn't my pastor's fault. He poured into me in ways no man had ever done—not my football coaches, my Army commanders, or my colleagues. He loved me like a father would a child. A devoted follower of Jesus, my pastor was humble and approachable. A servant-hearted guy to the core, Sam willingly went to the furthest lengths to meet my greatest needs.

How did I get to a place of wanting to avoid him, of wondering if I'd ever grow up in Christ, ever get beyond my struggles with sin, ever become the man I knew God wanted me to be?

I remembered our first discipleship meeting, sitting at my favorite coffee shop in downtown Oklahoma City. Even recalling that first hangout, I feel again how pumped I had been that day. I was a new believer, fresh out of the world and trying to get lost in the world of Love: life with Jesus. Maybe I was naïve, but I honestly believed it would be all growth and all joy, even through trials, from that day forward. How could it not be? I had Jesus. A wise and passionate man of God would be leading me in my spiritual journey. I eagerly anticipated living the kind of transformed life I saw in others.

But somewhere along the path, when it came to meeting up with my pastor, I started to feel like I imagine a criminal around his parole officer might feel. My once-great strides toward maturity had gradually dwindled like a dandelion going to seed in a warm spring breeze. This was the absolute opposite of the Paul-and-Timothy-type relationship Pastor Sam and I originally enjoyed. I started feeding him a lot of excuses (lies) about why I couldn't meet. He seemed confused but always acted with love and patience.

I was a man divided. Friends may have described me as a person of great integrity with humility, compassion, a strong character, and a radiant smile, but my family might have used words like egotistical, driven, distant, and self-obsessed. I was all smiles while my insides were going wild. Outwardly, I was the guy who busted his chops to serve. But I sacrificed to win the applause of people more than resting in God's love and acceptance. I might have been perceived as a man of self-discipline, but deep down I knew something wasn't right. There were nights I couldn't shake the dark mood of depression, so I'd stumble deeper into isolation, thinking that withdrawing from everything and everyone—including my pastor—would keep my internal battle hidden. Instead, it brought only unspeakable loneliness that tore at my soul.

Ambition, coupled with wanting to be known and seen, led me to a zealous desire to compete with others, even fellow Christians. Rivalry, comparison, and jealousy left me deflated like a slowly leaking balloon. I was plagued by hopelessness, restlessness, and the feeling that there was something more I had to do in order to be significant, valued, and loved.

I THANK GOD that Jesus didn't leave me in that place. The turn began at a worship service my wife, Denisse, and I attended. I had a powerful encounter with God the Holy Spirit that night. I finally had eyes to see my desperate need for the bright-burning flame of God's love. The gospel message of Jesus resounded in my soul like never before. Oh, how madly and passionately in love God is with me! From that moment on, I began to see my walk with Christ as a journey, not an end point. Sure, I hadn't "arrived," but that night it started to become clear: arrival wasn't the ultimate goal.

Open your heart to God's open heart as He reminds you that your destination is greater than your location. No matter how jaded your journey has been, it isn't over but is just starting.

The Bible repeatedly calls life with Jesus a walk. One of Christ's names is the Way (see John 14:6). In 1 Peter 2:11, Peter writes, "Beloved, I urge you as sojourners and exiles to abstain from the passions of the flesh, which wage war against your soul." Man, did I understand part of that verse. I definitely felt like an exile, with anger, intense lust, greed for greater wealth, resentment, and pride waging war against my soul. Trends constantly tempted me to compromise truth.

The part of that verse that took me longer to understand involved the word translated "sojourner." Not a term we use every day, right? Looking at the original Greek word, *paroikos*, we see this term can also be translated as a traveler, someone who journeys, a pilgrim.[1]

When you read *pilgrim*, don't think of guys in black hats with buckles on their shoes who landed at Plymouth Rock and displaced Native American tribes. Those dudes were called Pilgrims because they were travelers from a foreign land, separated from others because of their faith (the Pilgrims had been persecuted for Christ's name in their home country, England).

The Bible says we are travelers. Every day, we're on a journey with Jesus. Life with Christ is a walk, a pilgrimage. Here's what I began to discover: my discipleship meetings didn't create doubts; they just uncovered the pride, fear, and insecurity in me. *Will I ever change? What's wrong with me?*

Will it always be like this? I began to see that the walk of faith isn't linear. It's full of twists and turns, highs and lows.

In other words, it's like most journeys.

Almost everyone likes starting something. We also like arriving somewhere. We may have fun planning every detail of an awesome vacation and love finally getting to that destination, but who loves going through TSA at the airport? Who loves flat tires on a road trip, delays and lost luggage, cancellations and waiting in lines? "Getting there" is often the most difficult part of a journey.

THIS BOOK IS ALL ABOUT HOPE in the midst of the "getting there." It's about getting past your past so you can hold on to hope for the journey. It's also about moving to a closer connection with Jesus. In every chapter, we'll evaluate where we've been and where we're headed as we travel with God. We'll also look at how we can travel lightly, travel wisely, and travel together with our brothers and sisters in Christ. These five dynamics will form the foundation for each chapter.

In the difficult months before I began to embrace the reality of being on a journey with Jesus, I often felt like turning back to the life I used to know. I wanted to stop meeting with my pastor because I didn't have hope that things could really, truly change. I couldn't see how I could get from where I was to where God had called me to be.

If you've ever felt stuck in your walk with God, if you've ever felt like giving up, this book is for you. As an author, I debuted with a book titled *Start Where You Are*. Wherever you are, no matter how ugly a place, God invites you to start there—with anxiety, with bitterness, with anger. Once you've started where you are, Jesus begins to transform you from the inside out. This book is the logical next step. You've started where you are. Now it's time to press on and learn how to keep going.

You may have sung a beautiful song called "I Have Decided to Follow Jesus" at church. If you don't recognize the title, maybe the worship chorus will jog your memory. The refrain proclaims, "No turning back, no turning back." If you haven't heard this tune, I've put a link in the endnotes; you definitely want to look it up.[2]

The song originated in Assam, a state in far northeastern India. There, in the shadow of the Himalayas, the first Assamese converts were viciously persecuted by those who rejected Christ. A powerful legend has grown up about one of these first tribal converts, a man who was dragged before his tribe with wife and kids in tow. The clan leader demanded that he deny Jesus. The man refused. A warrior shot his wife, and, once again, the tribal leader ordered the new Christ-follower to recant his faith. Instead, the man began to sing a simple tune: "I have decided to follow Jesus, no turning back, no turning back."

The tribal warriors murdered his children, yet the man continued to sing, "The cross before me, the world behind me, no turning back, no turning back." Finally, the man himself fell as an arrow pierced his body. The words "no turning back" escaped his dying lips.[3]

I've named this book as both a call and a challenge. It's a call to the life of hope that a single focus on Jesus gives us.

And it's a challenge to leave behind—forever—our former lives, to get past our pasts. Travel with me as I travel with Christ. Jesus is the path and the prize, the way and the worthy one, the truth and the triumph you seek.

Let's go, my friend. No turning back.

From Forgetting Who You Were to Remembering Who You Are

Once you had no identity as a people; now you are God's people. Once you received no mercy; now you have received God's mercy.

1 PETER 2:10 NLT

AS MY FLIGHT DESCENDED, the rugged coastline of Mindanao came into focus. Home to jaw-dropping waterfalls, stunning surf beaches, amazing natural resources, and incredible biodiversity, Mindanao—the second largest Philippine island—was once dubbed "The Land of Promise."

It's also the poorest island in the Philippines and the site of ongoing terrorist attacks, kidnappings, piracy, and suffocating religious tension.

That day, I flew into Mindanao knowing full well that I'd soon enter a war zone. I had been invited to share the gospel on mission in the Philippines. I felt privileged, eager . . . and anxious. *It's about to get real,* my mind and heart hammered.

God has given me a great love for and deep connection with the Filipino people. My friends there—my brothers and sisters—are humble and God-fearing. I'm honored to work alongside them for Christ's glory.

It also completely freaked me out that we were headed to Marawi City the day after my arrival.

Rewind with me a bit to May 23, 2017, when militant jihadists attempted to seize control of Marawi City for ISIL, the Islamic State of Iraq and the Levant (sometimes known as ISIS). The most brutal armed conflict in the Philippines since World War II erupted in a city that literally crumbled under attack. Roughly 95 percent of the buildings within a 1.5-mile radius were heavily damaged or completely leveled. Radical terrorists ruthlessly executed dissenters, including Christians. Two hundred thousand people were displaced; evacuees died of dehydration in the desperate conditions of congested refugee camps. Shocking and horrifying, right? The Philippine government, with international support, waged war for five months. Two years of martial law followed, during which violence and threat festered just below the surface.

When my plane touched down, just over a year after the conflict ended, I knew Marawi City was still a chaotic place reeling from devastating destruction. I also knew I didn't have to go there.

After all, I hadn't flown to the Philippines only to share Jesus in Marawi; my mission extended beyond that one city. The outreach in Marawi could definitely happen without me, I reasoned. And a friend in nearby Iligan City had invited me to stay with him and his family. "Just chill with us," he urged. That sounded good to me!

I woke up the day after my arrival with my mind still racing, divided and unsure. Then God's voice broke through: *Rashawn, I called you here to be on mission for Me, not to lounge around, fluff pillows, and sleep. I want you to go in where others are running away.* I got ready and headed to the church where my Filipino friends had already gathered.

Walking into the church, I felt an amazing calm rush over me. I wasn't going in alone; brothers and sisters from all over the Philippine islands had arrived to share Christ in Marawi. Then, almost the next moment, I realized that I was at least a head taller than everyone else. I also stuck out like a sore thumb as the only "chocolate brotha" in the room. My skin was several shades darker than anyone else's. And whereas the Filipinos wore clothes that modestly covered every inch of skin, my thick, tattooed arms were quite noticeably bare. Saying I felt out of place would be a massive understatement.

By some miracle, a long-sleeved Manny Pacquiao Foundation jacket a Filipino pastor loaned me fit well enough, and, before I knew it, we had loaded the vans for the trip to Marawi. During the two-hour ride, I kept asking myself,

Can I really do this? Can I be like Paul, risking imprisonment and death for Jesus? Can I be like Stephen, being stoned to death for the sake of the gospel? Considering the number of martyrs in and around Marawi City, this was a genuine concern. I wanted to be brave; I knew God had called me. I clung to His peace and to Scripture verses He brought to mind, but as the time passed, my desire to turn back became more prevalent. I had to fight it with everything in me.

The leader of my group urged us to hide our Bibles (aka our spiritual swords) under the seats as we approached a military checkpoint. Men armed with gigantic automatic weapons drilled into us with searching eyes. But we were waved through by the guards and joyfully pressed on. The pastor asked me to crouch down as we entered the city, then wait in the van after our driver parked it next to a wall.

My incredibly brave sisters in Christ exited first, acting as decoys with scarves draped over their faces to distract from the tall black man—me—emerging at the Philippine equivalent of Ground Zero. Four brothers in Christ then surrounded me, shielding me from view, and ushered me into the home where three courageous Muslim families had gathered to talk about God. One of our Christian sisters had built relationships in this area for several years, and this was a marked moment: the invitation she had hoped to receive for so long to share the gospel.

Even though I had walked into the house, I felt like I had raced in a track meet. My whole body was tense as I passed through what felt like a movie scene. Then, barely catching my breath after climbing the squeaking, thin stairs, I was ambushed. Not by a militant, though; this was a little boy. "Whoa! Do you play in the NBA?" he shouted. "Are you LeBron James?" I couldn't stop cracking up like a worn-out shoe. God relieved my anxieties in that moment. Phew! The rest of the kids gathered around, the families settled in, and we had an amazing conversation that eventually led to Jesus. God moved in powerful ways, and what He did that day is still echoing in Marawi City.

I cannot tell you how grateful I am that I didn't give in to fear. That journey to Marawi was one of the most difficult of my ministry . . . maybe of my life. I honestly didn't know if I had what it took to risk all for Jesus. And the reality is, I didn't have it. In the past, I might have relied on my strength, my smile, and my charisma to get me through the fear, insecurity, and doubt. But I had come a long way from those days. I had walked with Christ for some years by the time I set foot in Marawi. I wasn't who I used to be and knew my identity was in Jesus. Only in Jesus.

On that trip, I faced the temptation not just to turn back to safety but to turn back to who I used to be—the Rashawn who never showed weakness, the Rashawn who could smile his way through anything, the Rashawn who impressed and influenced people for Rashawn's sake. I thank God that He gave me His strength to deny myself and press on, not just to Marawi and not just to share Him in a dangerous place but to journey further away from who I was and more completely into who I'm meant to be. I want that for you too, my friend.

WHERE WE'VE COME FROM

We all have a past. In some ways, that's not an earth-shattering statement; in other ways it's incredibly profound. Think about it: we've all come from somewhere. We all have a history. Everyone has a past that is deeply threaded with brokenness and beauty. We all have to decide what to do with our memories, our triumphs, our mistakes. We all have to answer the universal question, *Who am I?*

Whether we articulate it aloud or it simmers under the surface, we all deeply want to know, *Who am I?* It follows us from our very first moments.

As a baby, you were born into a world full of possibilities. You were called by a name. You may have been identified by a birth certificate and a lovingly married mother and father; you may have felt identified by abandonment. As you grew, you might have been identified as the honor student, the star athlete, the troubled kid, or the "good" Christian. You've been called names. You've been labeled and sorted and identified in countless ways.

If you're anything like me, you've struggled to know who you really are. Growing up, I only wanted to identify with my strengths: my football prowess, my online presence, my people skills. Like many reading this book, I did everything I could to hide my weaknesses. Who wants to be identified with failure and pain? Not me.

For so many years, I searched. I was on the same huge quest I see all over the world. *How can I be happy? Love myself more? Be the best version of myself?* Gurus tell us that the secret of happiness is to love and accept ourselves more;

this will allow us to be more successful, more complete. "Do you, Booboo," and all that.

What I've found—and maybe you've found this too—is that the promises of self-focus don't deliver. The more I fixated on self-improvement, the more aware I became that I wasn't getting all that much better. As I attached myself to the fulfillment of some mysterious and undefined "purpose" that people promised was "in me," I only became increasingly addicted to influence, affluence, success, and approval. What would satisfy me? What would finally make me feel good enough? What could possibly settle the nagging doubts about my worth? If money, a massive digital following, and more women than I could pay attention to couldn't make me happy, what on earth could?

The toxic culture of self-love will never satisfy. It can't. Why? Because creation can't fulfill or satisfy itself. Basing your identity on what you've done, who others say you are, or who you hope to be in the future only leads to crushing sorrow. It's just never enough. Apart from Christ, we aren't enough. As my beloved friend Allie Beth Stuckey would say, "You aren't enough, and that's okay."

We must escape the toxic culture of self-love. I'm not saying we shouldn't love ourselves, but truly loving ourselves only happens when we grow in awareness of God's love and His love frees and empowers us to love others. *It's a love that flees self-obsessing but flourishes in sacrifice. A love that isn't about self at all.*

Here's where I've come from: the world of bullies (foes) and groupies (fans). The bullies in my life tried to keep me down. Whether coming from actual people or the bullies inside my head, the words and lies about my identity used to tear me down faster than Usain Bolt can run. In order to compensate, I'd swing toward the groupies in my life, the people or thoughts that would puff me up and tell me how great I was. And like most of you, I'd much rather be identified with greatness than with weakness.

Right?

Have you experienced bullies or groupies telling you who you are? Maybe you've experienced way more of one than the other. You may have been so beat down by the words of others and your own insecurities that you think, *Man, it would be nice to have at least one groupie.* There's a trouble with listening to even one groupie, though: you and I can always find evidence that contradicts what a groupie says. For example, someone may write to me on social media: "Rashawn, you're awesome. I can't believe how many followers you have. You're doing so much for God's kingdom." Sure, this might give me a temporary ego shot in the arm. But I know the other side of that equation: there's always someone with more followers, there's always the possibility that my followers won't keep viewing or liking me, there's always more I could be doing—and there's the honest truth that people don't see the sin in my heart that Jesus is still sanctifying. If I let it, my mind could spin off what people would think if they watched me on a day I'm struggling with depression or temper or pride.

You and I live in a world of groupies and bullies. But the reality is, we don't have to listen to them. We don't have to identify with them. We don't need a foe or a fan—we need a friend who sticks closer than a brother. There is a better way.

WHERE WE'RE HEADED

Once I surrendered my life to Christ, I started a new quest. Now I'm no longer looking primarily for happiness, though I definitely enjoy being happy on earth and look forward to perfect happiness someday in heaven. I'm on a quest even more important than self-love, self-fulfillment, or self-improvement. It's a quest not simply to answer *Who am I?* but to live who I am.

Who I am was decided long ago: I am blessed by God in Christ with every spiritual blessing; chosen by Him before the foundation of the world; holy and blameless; predestined in love to be an adopted son and heir with Jesus; lavished with mercy, grace, and forgiveness; and part of God's eternal purpose to redeem and unite all things in Him, things in heaven and on earth. I didn't pull these words from nowhere. This is the glorious identity Ephesians 1:2–10 promises you and I can embrace.

No matter where you've come from, you're invited to glory in Jesus, with Jesus, like Jesus, forever. Our pursuit of happiness was never the answer to our identity problems; finding the Healer (Jesus) is. The Healer of our hurts creates beauty from our brokenness and makes us blessed and blameless. That's who we are in Him, forever.

Creation cannot fulfill or satisfy itself, but the Creator can fulfill and satisfy everything—including you—for all of eternity. He's already doing it, though our bound-by-time-and-space minds can take in only so much glory at one time. We see only moments of the story, but God sees the whole shebang. In fact, the Bible tells us He is "the Beginning and the End" (Rev. 1:8; 21:6; 22:13).

We have been called to identify with so much more and so much better than what we can grasp for ourselves. That's why the apostle Paul described his journey like this:

> Not that I . . . am already perfect, but I press on to make it my own, because Christ Jesus has made me his own. Brothers, I do not consider that I have made it my own. But one thing I do: forgetting what lies behind and straining forward to what lies ahead, I press on toward the goal for the prize of the upward call of God in Christ Jesus. (Phil. 3:12–14)

Like us, Paul did not perfectly live out his exalted identity in Christ. But he pressed on. He got past his past. He deliberately left behind his successes and his failures (read the rest of Philippians 3 to see the list of things he counted "worthless" compared to knowing Jesus). Paul urges us to likewise strain forward to what lies ahead: eternal life with Jesus.

Jesus is the path and the prize. So "let your eyes look directly forward, and your gaze be straight before you. Ponder the path of your feet; then all your ways will be sure" (Prov. 4:25–26). We have a heavenly citizenship and a glorious destination. Let's pursue them.

TRAVELING LIGHTLY

In order to press on, we've got to put off everything that might call us back to where we've been. We humans tend to gravitate back to who and where we were. Instead of viewing our past as a reference point, many of us try to make it our residence. We live in the past and wonder why we lack power in the present and fear the future. Beloved, don't stay there. Strain forward.

If we want to travel lightly, we have to put off our past identities and put on our new identity in Jesus alone.

Colossians 2:12 tells us that we have been "buried with [Jesus] in baptism, in which you were also raised with him through faith in the powerful working of God, who raised him from the dead." Romans 6:4 promises that, like Christ, "we too might walk in newness of life." To sum up: we all begin spiritually dead, but we don't have to stay there unless we want to.

I was a dead man before Jesus raised me to life. I had no heart for love. No eyes for light. No hope for everlasting life. Would I want to go back to that? Would I want to dig up someone who's dead? Excuse me for a second. . . . No way! There's no pleasure in exhuming a body, extracting a casket, or sifting through the dust and bones in a grave. I'm not trying to act crazy, but this is what it's like for us to go back to the cemetery of our past, to the days when we identified ourselves with the foolish things we do, the futile things we own, the fickleness of those we influence, the failings of what we've done, or the frustrations that come with who does or doesn't love us. For me, that identity is as dead as a doornail.

How about you?

Jesus tells us that we're seated with Him in a place of heavenly honor (see Eph. 2:6–7). I'm personally dazzled that the God of the universe would allow me access to Himself, let alone clothe me in His righteousness like Isaiah 61:10 promises.

Why would I want to rewind? I prefer to press play and strain forward in Christ. We don't stop dwelling on the past so we can attain heaven; it's already ours, promised and sealed forever! Nor do we, in Christ, stop turning back to our old ways so we can look like we've got it together. We can "walk in a manner worthy of the calling to which [we] have been called" because Jesus has already made us worthy (Eph. 4:1). In Jesus, we have nothing to prove and nothing to lose. Identity in Christ is ours to enjoy.

Some years ago, I remember reading an article about Apple genius Steve Jobs. Before his untimely passing, Jobs became known for many things: incredible creativity, savvy business acumen, compelling presentations . . . and wearing the same outfit. No matter how big or small the meeting, Jobs usually showed up in jeans, a fitted black turtleneck, and matching black shoes. For some, Steve Jobs became as identified with those clothes as he was with iPhones and MacBooks.

How weird would it have been if Steve Jobs had showed up at one of Apple's annual October conferences in a football jersey he'd worn in middle school, oversized pants, and fisherman sandals several sizes too big? Yeah; I'm pretty sure people'd be wiggin'.

Ill-fitting clothes can identify someone as quickly as Steve Jobs's sleek, turtlenecked appearance identified him. That's why you and I are invited to "put off your old self," your old identity, "which belongs to your former manner of life and is corrupt through deceitful desires" (Eph. 4:22). It no longer fits. Our pasts and our former ways of life no longer identify us.

The thing about identity is, there's no nakedness. If you put off one identity, you must take up another. There's no neutral answer when it comes to the question, Who am I? Fortunately, the Bible tells us not only what to put off but also what to put on.

TRAVELING WISELY

Our identity in Christ involves putting off the past with its ill-fitting rags of approval seeking, failure avoiding, and success grasping. If you're a Christian, that *old you* is dead. To travel wisely and well on this journey with Jesus, you've also got to put on your new identity, though. The book of Colossians uses the metaphor of clothing ourselves with new garments to describe putting on our identity in Christ.

> As God's chosen people, holy and dearly loved, clothe your-selves with compassion, kindness, humility, gentleness and patience. Bear with each other and forgive one another if any of you has a grievance against someone. Forgive as the Lord forgave you. (3:12–13 NIV)

Remember, Jesus is your path and your prize. Christ's fol-lowers are identified by His compassion, kindness, humility, gentleness, and patience. They forgive. They love as He has loved, and by this they are known as His disciples (see John 13:35).

Don't just put off your old ways; decide today—and every day to come—to put on your new self, your new nature, the clothes that perfectly fit a follower of Christ. One of the ways I learned to do this was by focusing on how the Bible answers the question Who am I? Scripture is full of "in Christ, I am" truths, including these:

- ▸ I am chosen (1 Thess. 1:4).
- ▸ I am treasured, honored, and loved (Isa. 43:4).
- ▸ I am accepted (Rom. 15:7).
- ▸ I am a new creation (2 Cor. 5:17).
- ▸ I am God's masterpiece (Eph. 2:10).
- ▸ I am more than a conqueror (Rom. 8:37).
- ▸ I am a child of the Most High God (John 1:12).
- ▸ I am free from condemnation and shame (Rom. 8:1; 10:11).
- ▸ I am a citizen of heaven (Phil. 3:20).

These truths don't just apply to me. This is your identity in Jesus too. And the statements above are just the beginning of a list that goes on and on, written by God, with love, from Genesis to Revelation. To help you discover more "who I am in Christ" affirmations, I've listed some helpful resources in the endnotes.[1]

You simply cannot live who you are without knowing who you are, and knowing who you are starts and ends with

Jesus Christ. As you put on His character—compassionate, kind, humble, gentle, patient, and forgiving—everything changes. Why would you go back to a closet full of grave-clothes when you can be robed in the righteousness of the King of Kings?

Traveling wisely means forgetting who you were, not because your past is completely irrelevant or unimportant but because it's only meant to be a reference point, the place from which your journey with Jesus begins. Forgetting who you were doesn't mean trying to erase the memories of your life before Christ; you and I both know that's not even humanly possible. Instead, it means choosing every day to remember what's eternally secure and what's most important: who you are in Christ is your firm foundation, triumphant truth, and only hope.

With David the warrior poet, let us pray,

> I love you, O LORD, my strength.
> The LORD is my rock and my fortress and my
>   deliverer,
>   my God, my rock, in whom I take refuge,
>   my shield, and the horn of my salvation, my
>   stronghold. (Ps. 18:1–2)

All too often we fail to go to the eternal Rock, then wonder why we can't find a firm place to stand. I've deliberately decided to stand on and in Christ, the unchanging Rock of Ages (see Heb. 13:8).

What about you? Will you pray, with the psalmist,

> Hear my cry, O God,
>> listen to my prayer;
> from the end of the earth I call to you
>> when my heart is faint.
> Lead me to the rock
>> that is higher than I,
> for you have been my refuge,
>> a strong tower against the enemy. (61:1–3)

Will you build your life on the shifting sand of success, approval, good looks, or a nice family? Or will you stake your claim on the Rock that is higher, the Truth that is greater, the Hope that is secure through every storm?

It's time. Don't hope you'll find out "who you are" someday. Decide you'll live out the truth of your identity in Christ today.

TRAVELING TOGETHER

Spend some time talking with God or discussing the following with an accountability partner or small group.

- ▸ Do you struggle to live with a thankful or peaceful heart? Read Colossians 2:6–7 and reflect on how these verses can help you.
- ▸ Do you have a bitter or hardened heart against those who have hurt you? Look back at Colossians 3:12–13 and notice the clothes that identify a Christ-follower. How does forgiveness fit with this picture?

▶ Do you regularly experience bouts of anger or use your words for gossip and slander? Read Luke 6:43–45. What kind of words identify a person who loves God?

▶ Do you find yourself passionately pursuing worldly things? Meditate on James 3:17–18 and Colossians 3:2. What pursuits—what the Bible calls "the things above"—identify authentic followers of Jesus?

POINTS TO PONDER AS YOU PROGRESS

God created your identity. Don't
allow the world to change it.

From Dirty Desires to Desiring God

Oh, taste and see that the LORD is good! Blessed is
the man who takes refuge in him!

PSALM 34:8

IF I HAD TURNED OFF THE HEADLIGHTS, the road in front of me would have disappeared. It was the kind of night best described as pitch black, and—as sad as I am to admit it—that night my heart mirrored the darkness outside. The speedometer pushed ninety as I barreled down the back roads between Lawrence and Topeka, Kansas, the car full of my rowdy, intoxicated friends.

When I was seventeen, what I wanted more than anything else was a good time. I was runnin' and gunnin', acting the fool, raising hell and taking others with me. As the wooded Kansas countryside zoomed past that night, I had no idea that my desire for "the high life" was about to come crashing down around me.

An unmistakable car pulled out of the inky darkness behind me. Its siren split the night, and the flashing reds and blues in my rearview mirror caused my stomach to sink.

"It's the po-po. . . . Quick! Roll down the windows," someone shouted.

Trying to expel the strong smell of marijuana from the car, desperate to figure out how I could get out of this one, I screeched to a halt on the shoulder. My lungs heaved with strained breath and my heart was pounding like a jackhammer as I watched the officer exit his vehicle. Not only had I been drinking and smoking, but I also didn't have my driver's license with me. All bad!

What I did have—and gladly gave to the police officer—was my brother's ID. Mashawn and I look enough alike that it might have worked, but things went from bad to worse when he ran the registration on the car I was driving. It never occurred to me that the car I'd borrowed might not have current tags and registration. To the officer who pulled me over, I must have looked like a drunken hoodlum speeding in a stolen car.

That night my desire for fun led to a three-hour roadside interrogation, lies mounting one on top of another, a trip to the county jail for fingerprinting, where the officer discovered my real identity, and a Breathalyzer test to determine whether I would be arrested for driving under the influence. Only by the grace of God was my blood alcohol level low that night, though I was high as a kite on marijuana. I didn't receive a DUI, but the consequences of my bent desires reached incredibly far.

The whole escapade cost me and my parents thousands of dollars. Mainly my parents. I lost friends overnight; parents who heard what had happened no longer wanted their kids to hang out with me. My reputation as an up-and-coming athlete was tarnished; some coaches viewed me as a troubled kid from that point forward. On a quest for a good time, I'd found out how completely damaging having the wrong desires can be. Sinful desires not only deceived me but destroyed me.

WHERE WE'VE COME FROM

Humans universally desire some things. We all hunger and thirst. We all long for safety and shelter. Most people also want to give and receive love, to find purpose and meaning in life, to be caught up in something grander and better than the daily grind. Humanity and desire are inextricably tied together.

The Bible tells us that desire comes from God. It's His design. "He himself gives to all mankind life and breath and everything," Acts 17:25 reveals. Just two verses later, the apostle Paul gives us the reason humans desire anything at all: "that they should seek God, and perhaps feel their way toward him and find him" (v. 27).

Think about it. God could have created us with no desires. He could have made our bodies completely self-sustaining, eliminating the desire for food, water, and sleep. He could have made our hearts self-contained, never needing attention or affection. But God didn't make us this way. He made us to long, to yearn, to seek to be found.

Our desires should point us to God, who gives life and breath and *everything*, just like Acts 17 declares. Maybe you've spotted a problem with this, though. Even if our desires should point us to God, they frequently deceive us. We often long for things that not only fail to lead us closer to God but also push us further from Him.

Like me, you've probably seen that some desires destroy us. Maybe you've watched a marriage explode because the desire for "sex on the side" set off a relationship grenade. Perhaps you've seen an alcohol, drug, food, or gambling addiction ruin someone's life. Maybe that life is yours. Your past desires may have poisoned your present. Even a desire that initially looks pretty "innocent"—wanting a good time, for instance—can lead to darkness in my heart and yours. The problem isn't that we desire; every person does. Trouble comes when our desires get out of order, and we desire anything more than we desire God.

What kind of story have your desires told? On your life's journey, where has longing taken you? If any desire displaces God at the center of your life, you're settling for something less than the glory for which you were created. C. S. Lewis says it this way: we were made for palaces, but we've settled for playing in the mud.[1] You and I come from the muck of dirty desires. Our longings have been bent and broken by sin.

Sin makes big promises . . . promises it never keeps. Sin promises gain but gives us loss. It promises freedom but sells us into slavery. Sin promises victory but keeps us in defeat. It promises life but delivers us unto death. As one of my favorite authors, Tim Chester, writes in his super helpful book *You Can Change: God's Transforming Power for Our Sinful Behavior and Negative Emotions,*

> Sin doesn't love us. It tries to use us, abuse us, enslave us, control us, and ultimately destroy us. Sin takes from us and gives nothing in return. It may use enticing and seductive lies. . . . But it's all lies. Sin never brings true and lasting satisfaction.[2]

When I was far from Christ, I indulged in anything and everything that brought me pleasure. I was a live-it-up, YOLO hedonist. Luke 12:19 sums up my attitude toward life: "And I will say to my soul, 'Soul, you have ample goods laid up for many years; relax, eat, drink, be merry.'" According to Ephesians 4:18, I wasn't alone; many people are "darkened in their understanding, alienated from the life of God because of the ignorance that is in them, due to their hardness of heart." When we delight in dirt rather than delighting in God, our hearts get hardened.

I'm so grateful that this time of overindulgence wasn't the end of my story. Dirty desires don't have to write your story either. Let's exchange our trash for His treasure. I found out quickly either the world's trash will keep you away from God's treasure or God's treasure will keep you away from the world's trash.

In Christ, your journey can lead to a better place.

WHERE WE'RE HEADED

If sin puts us on a path of destruction, where does desiring God take us? The Bible gives a clear answer. While "the desires of the flesh and the desires of the eyes and pride of life [are] not from the Father but [are] from the world . . . whoever does the will of God abides forever" (1 John 2:16–17). In today's language, we might say that whoever does what God wants is golden. Follow Jesus, long for Him more than anything else, and you're set forever.

Sinful pride and broken desire push the love of God out of our hearts. That's why John tells us so clearly: "Do not love the world or the things in the world. If anyone loves the world, the love of the Father is not in him" (v. 15). But here's the amazing thing: the reverse is far truer and more powerful. Not only does the love of God expel sinful desire but Christ's love also transforms it.

If we accept His gift of grace, God removes our old hearts, hardened by sin, and gives us His heart instead. He propels us past our pasts. God's love reminds us that we're never too dirty to be cleansed, never too far to be found, never too broken to be loved and accepted . . . unconditionally. Our desires are changed by the love of God.

I love how pastor John Piper explains this: "Conversion is the creation of new desires, not just new duties; new delights, not just new deeds; new treasures, not just new tasks."[3] That's why he encourages us to "pray for new taste buds on the tongue of your heart."[4] Amen, brother.

I started this chapter with words from Psalm 34:8: "Oh, taste and see that the LORD is good! Blessed is the man who takes refuge in him!" When we savor the pleasures of God, we cannot help but love Him more. And when we love Jesus, we begin to treasure Him above any other desire; we delight in Him more than any earthly joy. Love and desire for God reinforce one another in amazing ways. I long for new taste buds on the tongue of my heart, and I pray that for you too. It's not just a good way to live; it's *the* way.

The great Bible commentator Matthew Henry wrote, way back in 1708, "The joy of the Lord will arm us against the assaults of our spiritual enemies and put our mouths out of taste for those pleasures with which the tempter baits his hooks."[5] Consider this with me: that sentence was written over three hundred years ago, but its truth is as solid in the 2020s as it was then. God's joy is our offense and defense; it protects us against the attacks of the enemy and allows us to fight the temptations that the lust of the eyes and the lust of the flesh present. Not only do we develop new taste buds that desire God as we love Him more but our mouths are also "put out of taste" for worldly pleasures.

If you commit to following Jesus Christ, you aren't signing up for a life of drudgery. In fact, the Bible makes staggering promises about the delights of desiring God, such as in Psalm 16: "You make known to me the path of life; in your presence there is fullness of joy; at your right hand are pleasures forevermore" (v. 11). *Come on!* Fullness of joy, pleasure forever, real and lasting life—isn't that what we all want?

The Bible tells us that, if His life-giving, joyful presence is where we long to head, the path before us is clear: "Seek first the kingdom of God and his righteousness, and all these things will be added to you" (Matt. 6:33). In other words, when you make the kingdom of God your primary focus, your greatest desires, along with everything else, will fall into place.

We've got to put first things first if we want to get second and third things thrown in. Temporary pleasures can be taken away; happiness only lasts so long. Joy in God, though, can never be taken away. Because no human or thing gives us our joy in Christ, no person or thing can take it from us. While happiness is about living it up today, joy in Jesus stretches into eternity. It isn't just about the here and now; it's for both now and forever.

As amazing as this world is—and God did a phenomenal job in creating it—the earth is broken because of sin. We can't rely on the here and now or set our hopes and desires on it, because our world is fading away. It's on the way out. Hebrews 1:10–12 confirms this powerfully:

> You, Lord, laid the foundation of the earth in the
>   beginning,
>   and the heavens are the work of your hands;
> they will perish, but you remain;
>   they will all wear out like a garment,
> like a robe you will roll them up,
>   like a garment they will be changed.
> But you are the same,
>   and your years will have no end.

Your favorite clothes eventually wear out. Man, I hate that. Those shoes I love get stained; my favorite shirt fades in the wash. Like old clothes, this world is breaking down—and disappointing us as it does. Only God never fails; "Jesus Christ is the same yesterday and today and forever" (13:8).

With new taste buds on the tongues of our hearts, we're headed to the feast Christ sets before us.

> How precious is your steadfast love, O God!
>   The children of mankind take refuge in the
>   shadow of your wings.
> They feast on the abundance of your house,
>   and you give them drink from the river of your
>   delights.
> For with you is the fountain of life;
>   in your light do we see light. (Ps. 36:7–9)

Are you ready for the banquet? Let's go!

TRAVELING LIGHTLY

The Psalms are full of expressions of desire. I love that. They're so real and raw. Some of the words are super convicting for me. Take Psalm 27:4, for instance: "One thing have I asked of the LORD, that will I seek after: that I may dwell in the house of the LORD all the days of my life, to gaze upon the beauty of the LORD and to inquire in his temple." I don't know about you, but I've asked for more than one thing over the course of my life.

Yet I want to want what the psalmists express:

> O God, you are my God; earnestly I seek you;
>   my soul thirsts for you;

my flesh faints for you,
> as in a dry and weary land where there is no
> water.
So I have looked upon you in the sanctuary,
> beholding your power and glory.
Because your steadfast love is better than life,
> my lips will praise you.
So I will bless you as long as I live;
> in your name I will lift up my hands.
My soul will be satisfied as with fat and rich food,
> and my mouth will praise you with joyful lips.
> (63:1–5)

Wow. These are powerful, no-turning-back words.

If that's where we want to go, we've got to shut the door on dirty desires. We've got to suffocate any worldly longings we used to cultivate, transferring our attention and affection to Christ alone.

One day when I was in high school, I took our dog for a neighborhood walk. This dog was fired up to be outside. He was living his best life, sniffing here, there, and everywhere. Then his attention locked onto a black shape in the distance. Without a moment's hesitation, the dog bolted—and I'm talking full-throttle bolted—down the street. The leash flew out of my hands, and I raced after the dog, hoping the cat, or whatever it was, would get away unscathed.

To my horror, I realized I should have been praying my dog would get away unscathed. You see, that black shape turned out to be a skunk. And, as you probably guessed, it defended itself as all skunks do.

Sprayed from head to paw, my dog seemed dazed and confused at first, anxiously rubbing his eyes with his paws, desperate to escape the scent. Before I knew it, though, my dog got a better idea: to head back home. My terror multiplied when I remembered that, thinking we'd only be gone for a few minutes, I'd left the front door of our house standing open. I knew without a shadow of a doubt if that fool of a dog got inside, my mom would be speaking in tongues with no need for interpretation. You feel me?

I ran with everything in me, and I would have bested that dog—if I hadn't tripped in the front yard. Sprawled on the grass, I watched as that skunk-sprayed beast bounded up the steps and into our front room. It's honestly a miracle I lived to tell this tale. (Okay, so maybe not a full-fledged miracle, but let's just say that what I had imagined wasn't too far off when it came to my mom freaking out.)

That dirty dog wreaked havoc in our house. And I trust that you've seen dirty desires wreak havoc in your heart too. Just like I should have shut the door of our house, we've got to shut the door of our hearts to the out-of-order desires that infect us.

In Luke's Gospel, Jesus gives us a powerful word picture for this:

Your eye is the lamp of your body. When your eye is healthy, your whole body is full of light, but when it is bad, your body is full of darkness. Therefore be careful lest the light in you be darkness. If then your whole body is full of light, having no part dark, it will be wholly bright, as when a lamp with its rays gives you light. (11:34–36)

In other words, what comes in through our eyes leads to light or darkness. Our eyes are like a gateway. It's true that we're sometimes exposed to things we wish we'd never seen and never would have chosen. A lot of what enters our hearts through the gateway of our eyes does boil down to our choices, though. If we look at dark things, darkness will fill us.

In the days before my commitment to desire God above everything else, I let in a whole lot of darkness. I watched porn, thinking that was the popping thing to do. I also watched terribly violent videos on social media and You-Tube. I consumed massive amounts of darkness in the name of entertainment.

Sadly, because of traumatic experiences in my past, I cultivated bent desires through what I watched. I had been shot and left for dead as a teenager, so even though they haunted me, I watched video after video of people being gunned down. Being forced to watch sexual brutality as a child had twisted my desire for sex, a desire God originally designed to be pure, good, and holy. Watching porn didn't heal the wounds of my past; it allowed more darkness into my heart through the gateway of my eyes.

It's time to cast off dark entertainment in the name of Jesus. Amen? Don't allow what you binge-watch, click on, or post pervert the clean heart Christ died to give you. *That'll preach!*

Don't surrender to the desires of your former self, the bent and sinful desires that infect us. Sometimes we relive a traumatized past through what we watch. I've chosen and urge you to choose not to be held hostage by dark desires from the past. The Bible calls us to flee the darkness of sinful passions (see 2 Tim. 2:22).

Hebrews 11:24–26 gives us a strong example of desiring God more than anything else:

> By faith Moses, when he was grown up, refused to be called the son of Pharaoh's daughter, choosing rather to be mistreated with the people of God than to enjoy the fleeting pleasures of sin. He considered the reproach of Christ greater wealth than the treasures of Egypt, for he was looking to the reward.

God didn't tell Moses to desire nothing. He told him to keep his eyes on the real prize. Moses knew that at God's right hand were pleasures forever. Like Moses, we need to count the pleasures of heaven as greater than any pleasure the world can offer. And what's great is the pleasures of God *actually are greater*. We don't have to "convince ourselves." We're simply invited to taste and see.

If we want to travel the path of life lightly and freely, we must shut the door to dirty desires. We're also called to shut the door on "stinkin' thinking." Enter the door of God's joy and delight; lock it up in your mind. This is so important that I've devoted the entire next chapter to how transformed thinking eradicates toxic lies in our minds and hearts. For now, just keep in mind that, in the same way that allowing darkness through our eyes bends and breaks us, allowing darkness into our thoughts poisons us too.

So we cast off dark entertainment and shut the door on toxic thoughts in the name of and for the sake of Jesus

Christ. We pray for new taste buds on the tongues of our hearts and new tunes on the drums of our ears. We seek first the kingdom and trust Him to add everything else to us. We keep our eyes on the real prize, and we also cast off the community of darkness that might drag us back to dirty desires.

Psalm 1 describes this perfectly:

> Blessed is the man
>> who walks not in the counsel of the wicked,
> nor stands in the way of sinners,
>> nor sits in the seat of scoffers;
> but his delight is in the law of the LORD,
>> and on his law he meditates day and night.
> He is like a tree
>> planted by streams of water
> that yields its fruit in its season,
>> and its leaf does not wither.
> In all that he does, he prospers.
> The wicked are not so,
>> but are like chaff that the wind drives away.
> Therefore the wicked will not stand in the
>> judgment,
>> nor sinners in the congregation of the righteous;
> for the LORD knows the way of the righteous,
>> but the way of the wicked will perish.

I've spent far too many hours walking with the wicked, standing with sinners, and sitting with scoffers. Man, I wish I had some of that time back. I look back at the me speeding in Kansas so many years ago and see how much like chaff I was, driven away from God by the winds of sinful pleasure—which at that time proved to be a fatal distraction from the goodness of God. It wasn't only on that night that broken desire led me to judgment and close to death. Wrong desires really, truly do lead to destruction.

If we're going to cast off a community that celebrates dirty desires, reject toxic thoughts, and shut the door on dark entertainment, we've got to have a plan for what we will do . . . and how we'll do it. Let's look now at how we can travel wisely on the road of godly desire.

TRAVELING WISELY

The Gospel of Luke warns us against allowing darkness into our hearts. It also promises that "if then your whole body is full of light, having no part dark, it will be wholly bright, as when a lamp with its rays gives you light" (11:36). I thank God that He doesn't make finding light a mystery. Psalm 119:105 clearly reveals where the light is found. "Your word," O Lord, "is a lamp to my feet and a light to my path." Desiring God and desiring His Word lead to light and life.

If you want to travel wisely, let the Word guide your every step. The Message paraphrase renders Psalm 119:5–6 as a helpful prayer: "Oh, that my steps might be steady, keeping to the course you set; then I'd never have any regrets in comparing my life with your counsel." We can get past our pasts and eradicate shame when we live according to the light of God's Word.

Traveling wisely means both reading the Word of God and allowing it to read us. As we receive more and more of the light of Jesus's truth, corners of our minds and hearts that have held on to darkness are cleansed and set free. I've recently been doing some deep cleaning in my heart, and I encourage you to do the same. Confession and repentance are natural responses to the light of God's Word.

In a perfect world, we'd be able to go through every day thinking only clean thoughts. You and I both know we don't live in that perfect world, though. Far from it! That's why God gives us verses like Philippians 4:8 to help us discern between dirty desires and pure ones: "Whatever is true, whatever is honorable, whatever is just, whatever is pure, whatever is lovely, whatever is commendable, if there is any excellence, if there is anything worthy of praise, think about these things."

Think about these things—true, honorable, just, pure, lovely, commendable things. Excellent things, things worthy of praise. It's not rocket science: when we think about "these things," our tastes change, our desires change, and our lives change.

What things are you thinking about? Allow me to suggest that you take some time to evaluate that. Are you delighting in the law of the Lord, like we read the righteous person of Psalm 1 does? Are you cultivating the joy of the Lord that is your strength (see Neh. 8:10)? Do you treasure and desire God above everything else?

Remember, either the love of God transforms the desires of your heart, or the love of the world crowds out the love of God. If we don't fix our eyes on Jesus, our taste buds won't change. If we don't choose *the way*, we'll drift away.

"Therefore," Hebrews commands, "we must pay much closer attention to what we have heard, lest we drift away from it. . . . How shall we escape if we neglect such a great salvation?" (2:1, 3). There is nothing greater than the salvation Jesus Christ purchased for us on the cross of Calvary. May we never neglect it but allow it instead to take us from dirty desires to desiring God.

TRAVELING TOGETHER

Spend some time talking with God or discussing the following with an accountability partner or small group.

- ► Are you currently compromising your faithfulness to God to indulge yourself in the pleasures of the world? Look carefully at your mind, heart, and actions.
- ► Read Matthew 14:22–33. Peter wanted to walk on water. He desired a great thing. What happened when he took his eyes off Jesus? Nobody puts their hopes in a company destined to go bankrupt. Nobody deliberately gets on a sinking ship. This world is passing; it's going bankrupt; the ship is sinking. Why do you think anyone would choose to stay on a sinking ship?
- ► Read Galatians 6:8–9: "For the one who sows to his own flesh will from the flesh reap corruption, but the one who sows to the Spirit will from the Spirit reap eternal life. And let us not grow weary of doing

good, for in due season we will reap, if we do not give up." How does the truth of this passage fit with the chapter you just read?

▶ Have you prayed that God would give you new taste buds on the tongue of your heart? If not, you can start now!

POINTS TO PONDER AS YOU PROGRESS

God never exposes our dirt to be a killjoy, but He has promised to get rid of things that kill our joy in Him.

From Toxic Thinking
to Transformative Truth

You will know the truth, and the truth will set you free.

JOHN 8:32

A LIGHT MIST ROSE from the lake that October morning. It was the perfect fall day to meet my good friend Dennis for a prayer walk—crisp, invigorating, aflame with autumn color. We set out around the lake, talking to and about God, giving Him praise, and sharing what each of us was learning from Scripture. We quickly discovered both of us had been meditating on the psalms, particularly Psalm 119.

Dennis is a young man fired up for the Lord. He exudes the kind of passion for God that draws people closer to Jesus. All the time! As Dennis reflected on Psalm 119 that morning, he told me why hiding God's Word in his heart, rejecting the darkness that creeps into our journey, and living out truth mattered to him so much. It all started for him in childhood. I'll let him tell you his story . . .

When I was in grade school, my mom always got after me to read more. I was definitely more interested in sports than in books, especially basketball, but Mom pestered me so much that I finally gave in and went to the library to pick out a book. When I got to the library, I realized I had no idea what to read. And there were just so many books.

One title finally caught my eye: *The Devil's Court*. A book about a kid who loves basketball. All right; that I could do. I took the book home and was surprised how much I liked it. I kept wanting to read. I was fascinated by the main character and what was happening in his life. To sum up, he meets the devil, who promises that he can help this boy make every single shot . . . for the rest of his life. No more misses. The kid basically sells his soul to the devil to become a better basketball player.

I was young and didn't totally understand everything I was reading. I definitely didn't comprehend the super serious spiritual implications of it. I had been raised with some faith, but the truth hadn't taken root in me. I just couldn't stop thinking about the deal this kid made. My mind spun with questions: What if I never missed another shot? Could I make a deal with the devil? Would selling my soul make me a better athlete? Maybe like Kobe Bryant or Michael Jordan? Ayeee!

I was thinking these thoughts. Actually, I was obsessed with them.

So, underneath my breath one day, I asked for the deal. Thank God Jesus protected me from myself. The very next shot I took bricked violently—a lot like Shaquille O'Neal at a free throw line. And the one after that, and so on . . . and so on. Being as young as I was, my only thought was, *Man, it didn't work.* I didn't try to make another deal. I just figured the whole idea had been made up for the book and went on with my life. I definitely didn't think I might need to ask God's forgiveness for what I had done, for what I had thought and believed.

I look back on that me, that young boy who had no clue how dangerous thinking about and dwelling on the wrong things could be. I wish so much I would have known back then that what you think about changes you . . . big time. It never crossed my mind that some library book could introduce me to ideas that might have shaped my eternal future were it not for the grace of God.

That's why I stay close to God's Word. Like closer than close. I may be forced to socially distance myself from people but not the precious promises of God. I know how easily darkness can come waltzing into my mind. But I want to walk in the light of truth, and that starts with thinking about God as I go about my day. Like David, I've tasted and seen the goodness of God (Ps. 34:8).

I'm not turning back.

WHERE WE'VE COME FROM

When people first come to Jesus, they often focus on changing their behavior. They want to stop doing some things and start doing others. Even if they don't realize it. The reality is, no matter how many years someone has known Christ, it's tempting to fixate on what we do or don't do, mostly ignoring what we *think*.

This is disastrous.

Think I'm exaggerating? Think again.

Why do you do what you do? Why don't you do certain things? It all starts with your thoughts, your core beliefs. Our actions are in no way random. Not at all. They spring from what we regularly think.

For example, if a person thinks success is the most important thing in life, that person may become super hardworking or greedy. One of these behaviors obviously looks more positive than the other on the outside, but both actions are the logical outcome of *thinking* about success—the worldly kind. If a person believes romantic love is the most important thing, he or she may dive into a lot of DMs on social media or become a serial dater on apps like Tinder or Christian Mingle, always looking for the perfect partner but never satisfied, because everyone eventually disappoints. Again, evaluating actions—lots of chatting online or lots of dating, for instance—is important to a certain degree, but what's really driving that behavior is a series of thoughts and beliefs, perhaps along these lines: *If I find love, then I'll feel complete.*

Bottom line: on your journey with Jesus, what you think is incredibly important. When the Bible talks about sin, it's talking about both sinful actions *and* sinful thoughts. Check out what the apostle Paul says about this in Ephesians 4:17–18:

Now this I say and testify in the Lord, that you must no
longer walk as the Gentiles do, in the futility of their minds.
They are darkened in their understanding, alienated from
the life of God because of the ignorance that is in them, due
to their hardness of heart.

Do you see how God uses Paul's words to connect action
and belief? When people are separated from Jesus, they
walk (act) "in the futility of their minds." In the New Living Translation, the Greek words used by Paul to describe
people's thoughts are translated as "hopelessly confused"
(v. 17). The Passion Translation speaks of "empty delusions"
(v. 17). "Their corrupted logic has been clouded . . . deep-
seated moral darkness keeps them from the true knowledge
of God" (v. 18 TPT).

Here's what's crazy. You can be morally decent. You can
attend church. You can even do all the "right" Christian
things—float around and have manna for breakfast—and
still live an ungodly life. How? By never allowing Jesus to
transform your thinking. When we live our everyday lives
with no thoughts of God or His will—even if we're "good
people" doing "good things"—we miss the mark. A God-
centered (rather than me-centered) life starts in the mind.

The ultimate goal of our journey isn't simply to live a
respectable life. A moral life without a mind fixed on God
will never take us where we need to be: deeper into His glory
and goodness. Life is measured not only by our actions but
also by our mindset.

Honestly, I rub shoulders all the time with some of the
hardest working, most respectable, and most generous

people. They also live with God far from their thoughts. Some of them even attend church once a week but then go about the rest of the week as if God doesn't exist. They aren't "bad people" committing overtly wicked works, but they are ungodly. Why? Because God isn't part of their daily thoughts.

Man, I've been there, and I'm never going back to that.

So let me ask you: How often do you think of God as you journey through life? As believers, we've got to be honest about where we've been and where we go in our minds. Yeah, I know. It's kind of scary. But *assessing* our thought patterns and *addressing* them accordingly is a foundational part of *advancing* in our walk with Jesus.

A lot of us, even committed believers, are stuck in and tempted by old, sinful patterns because of the toxic thoughts we entertain. We may wake up and read the Bible. We may listen to worship music or do some other spiritual thing. If the first thing or many things that happen after this refreshing appointment with God include disappointment, anxiety, or anger, our minds may not be as fixed on Christ as we'd like them to be.

Toxic thoughts keep us living in what the prominent pastor Paul David Tripp calls "functional atheism." He writes,

> Yes, we believe that God exists, that he created the heavens and the earth, that the Bible is accurate, and that paradise awaits, but we often live—at a functional level—as if there is no God. We worry too much. We control too much. We demand too much. We regret too much. We run after God replacements too much. We do all these things because

we have forgotten God's presence, power, and glory. If you look around and look at yourself, you'll see evidence of functional atheism everywhere in the lives of Christians. This week, how many thoughts did you have, words did you speak, or decisions did you make that omitted the Lord from your process entirely?[1]

When we terminate God from our thoughts, toxicity is bound to dominate our lives.

If, like me, you've sometimes lived excluding God from your thoughts, it's time for a change. Inside out. It's time to deliberately decide to live with God not only on our minds but also in and through *His* heart! We are called to be godly; our lives should be lived out in His presence, with eyes, ears, lips, hands, feet, and thoughts that are pleasing to Him. The cross before us, the world behind us!

WHERE WE'RE HEADED

Okay, so we're interested in thinking rightly, not just acting rightly. What's the next step? How do we actually fix our minds on God and keep our thoughts there? We find a clue in observing what makes true Christ-followers different from their nice, decent, but unbelieving neighbors.

It all starts with truth. A Christian believes that God created humankind, people chose (and still choose!) sin, Jesus died to pay the just penalty for that sin, and our resurrected Lord will one day welcome His followers home to eternal life with Him. Dwelling on and living out these core gospel truths transform us from people who do good things into redeemed saints who've been set free from sin.

Jesus promises that, in Him, "[we] will know the truth, and the truth will set [us] free" (John 8:32). Freedom in Christ means we not only live differently but also think differently.

We have been freed; now we can see.

Remember how Ephesians 4:18 said you and I were living with darkened understanding and hardened hearts? Romans 6:17 furthers this point by telling us we "used to be slaves to sin" (NIV). The freedom we receive from Jesus transforms us from living in sin's confinement to the spacious, set-apart life in Him. God's perfect sovereignty and His unfailing love for us have been revealed in truth, truth that sets us free. However, we will never live in truth if we don't remain in Him and He in us (see John 15:1–5). We remain in Him by turning our thoughts—over and over, every day—to the God who died that we might be free.

Esteemed theologian A. W. Tozer once commented, "What comes into our minds when we think about God is the most important thing about us."[2] Wow! How true is that? If we think darkened, untrue thoughts about God, we'll never experience or live in His truth that sets us free. But if we know His truth and deliberately live in it, we'll be transformed from the inside out. It won't just be our actions that look good; our minds will be changed. So will our hearts.

Take a quick look back at Ephesians 4:17–18 with me:

> Now this I say and testify in the Lord, that you must no longer walk as the Gentiles do, in the futility of their minds.

They are darkened in their understanding, alienated from the life of God because of the ignorance that is in them, due to their hardness of heart.

Trace the progression here . . . futile thoughts and darkened understanding go with a hardened heart and ignorance. Ouch. I don't want that to be true of me, and I imagine you don't either.

The Old Testament book of Ezekiel speaks to this same issue and makes an astonishing promise about hope for hardened hearts. God proclaims,

And I will give you a new heart, and a new spirit I will put within you. And I will remove the heart of stone from your flesh and give you a heart of flesh. And I will put my Spirit within you, and cause you to walk in my statutes and be careful to obey my rules. (36:26–27)

God will transform our hardened hearts and, through His Spirit in us, cause us to walk in His ways. In order to walk in His ways, we have to know His statutes and rules; that's the right-thinking piece of this equation. I also don't want you to miss this crucial dynamic: God vows to put all this in us; it's not based on what you or I can do . . . ever. It's not about what we can pull off but who God places in us: His Holy Spirit. The supernatural movement of the Holy Spirit works this extraordinary change deep within us, turning our toxic thinking to transformative truth.

The Lord furthers this point in another mind-blowing declaration through the prophet Isaiah: "You keep him in perfect peace whose mind is stayed on you, because he trusts in you" (26:3). Think about that for a second. *Perfect peace.* A mind free of anxious, bitter, and/or insecure thoughts. Freedom from shame. *Perfect peace.*

If where we've been is imprisoned by clouded thinking and corrupted logic, here's where the journey is headed for those who follow Christ: freedom through truth, a new heart, fullness in the Spirit, and perfect peace. C'mon. Who doesn't want this? No matter where we've been, this is where we can go. And it starts in our minds. We must fight daily to abstain from the passions of our old, controlled-by-the-flesh ways and instead pursue the way of the One who is truth. Only then will our lives be made new. It's time to get past the thought patterns of our pasts.

It's often frustrating for me that the dismantling of my old self, with all its toxic thoughts, is not immediate. It's progressive. It takes time to grow in godliness, and we must be set apart in our thinking. But when Jesus becomes a person we know, and not just a place we go for help, everything will change . . . especially how we think.

Let's look now at some things we can deliberately put off as we journey with Jesus. As we travel lightly and freely in our minds, we'll experience more and more of His perfect peace.

TRAVELING LIGHTLY

I love to take morning prayer walks. In fact, if you follow me on social media, you'll see that I often record videos before or after these sacred times with God. I may walk with my iPhone, but I'll tell you what I don't walk with: a ball and chain. Sounds ridiculous, I know, but hear me out. There's a whole lot of Christians walking around chained to toxic thoughts. Instead of our minds being a *palace*, filled with the timeless truths in Christ we treasure, we at times allow them to become a *prison*, overpopulated with toxic thoughts we hate or tolerate.

I know this is true, because I was there. *Have you ever been imprisoned in your own mind?* Be honest. I confess; I'm guilty! For this reason, I'm thankful for the testimony of Brother Yun, a Chinese house church leader who was locked in prison—an actual prison—yet still eluded the utter temptation of toxic thinking. He once fervently wrote about the time he spent imprisoned for faithfully proclaiming the gospel of Jesus Christ, saying, "The prison was a reality, but Jesus was the truth!"[3] Brother Yun gives us a fine example of what it looks like to cherish the truth and cancel toxicity even in troubling times. He may have been chained according to people, but he was free according to God. In essence, it doesn't matter if you're locked down in a prison you can see (an actual prison) or can't see (your mind). When Jesus is your truth, freedom becomes your reality.

As I mentioned in the last chapter, if we're going to live no-turning-back lives for Jesus, we've got to put off the weight of toxic thoughts and take on the mind of Christ. The Bible tells us this is a battle. In 2 Corinthians 10:4–6, the apostle Paul uses military imagery to describe how followers of God wage war against toxic thinking. In Christ, "We destroy arguments and every lofty opinion raised against the knowledge of God, and take every thought captive to obey Christ" (v. 5). Like soldiers on a righteous mission, we launch deliberate campaigns against every deceptive thought that threatens our freedom.

When I was first learning to walk in the truth, I found help and guidance in Dr. Neil Anderson's book *Victory over the Darkness: Realizing the Power of Your Identity in Christ*. Dr. Anderson makes some simple and profound statements in his chapter "Winning the Battle for Your Mind."

> The more time and energy you invest in contemplating your own plans on how to live your life, the less time and energy you have to seek God's plan. You begin flip-flopping back and forth between acknowledging God's plan and leaning on your own understanding. James called this kind of person double-minded, "unstable in all his ways" (James 1:8). When you continue to vacillate between God's plan A and your plan B, your spiritual growth will be stunted, your maturity in Christ will be blocked, and your daily experience as a Christian will be marked by disillusionment, discouragement, and defeat.[4]

I don't know anyone who wants to sign up for disillusionment, discouragement, and defeat. We want the freedom Christ died to give us, right? Dr. Anderson identifies that *time* is a key component in transforming our thinking. In other words, if we want renewed minds, we have to put in the time. God doesn't enact a control-alt-delete reboot of our brains when we come to know Him. Instead, He invites us to participate in the process by investing our thoughts in His Word, His eternal purposes, His goodness, and His glory. The reverse is also true: if we invest more time contemplating our own plans or the world's ways, our minds will be formed in that image.

Which is currently true of you? Do you spend more time focused on the thoughts of God and taking lies captive to Christ, or do you spend your time focused on what you do or don't have? Even seemingly religious thoughts can become toxic if we focus on what God has or hasn't given us, whether we're better or worse than the people around us, or why this or that has happened or not. Are you picking up what I'm putting down here?

In order to travel lightly, we need to choose not only where to focus our thoughts (away from self and onto our glorious God) but also *how much* time we'll spend on certain kinds of thoughts. We also need to identify and follow a biblical pattern for Christ-honoring thinking. Let's look at that now.

TRAVELING WISELY

In order to win the battle in our minds and experience the freedom of living in truth, you and I need to develop a strategy. And that strategy has to start with exposing lies. Reality is, many of us have a whole lot of lie-residue built up in our brains. We lived and believed in certain ways before we met and received Christ, and the scum of stinkin' thinking clings to the corners of our minds. Escaping that past starts with knowing the truth better and better each day.

Since the enemy of God "is a liar and the father of lies" (John 8:44), we know that deception, falsehoods, manipulations of truth, and half-truths are all part of his strategy. And I assure you: the enemy doesn't play fair. His entire aim is "to steal and kill and destroy" (10:10). What a lot of Christians don't consider is that the enemy doesn't have to physically kill or destroy us, nor steal our possessions, if he can get to us through our thoughts. He can influence our entire lives—and destroy us in the process—by infecting our thinking.

That's why the primary strategy for a godly life is knowing truth and living it out. Again, using military imagery, Ephesians 6 teaches us how to wage war against "the schemes of the devil" by putting on "the belt of truth" and wielding "the sword of the Spirit, which is the word of God" (vv. 11, 14, 17).

If you want the freedom of truth, you've got to *know* truth. "Let the word of Christ dwell in you richly," Colossians 3:16 declares. Savor the Word. Indulge in it. Let it flood you with all wisdom. Eugene Peterson paraphrased this verse in a very helpful way: "Let the Word of Christ— the Message—have the run of the house. Give it plenty of room in your lives" (Message).

When we give the truth full run of our house, when we give it plenty of room in our lives, we have less and less space for lies. The ultimate aim is to have zero room for lies.

Before I knew Jesus as Lord and Savior, I had no hunger for His Word. I didn't know I was chained to toxic thinking, though I could see the results of it in my life—overusing alcohol, weed, porn, sex, and every other distraction I could think of. I didn't realize I was chasing after all of that because I had bent thoughts and false beliefs. I tried to start or stop doing things, but I still felt defeated. I didn't realize I had to look at my thought life.

When I started meditating on and memorizing Scripture, though, I saw how God's Word shapes the way we view the world and conforms our minds to His viewpoint. The Word leads us to a deeper understanding of His purpose for our lives. Memorizing God's Word makes His truth more accessible and usable when we're confronted with temptations. It enables us to discern between truth and falsehood.

Meditating on and memorizing Scripture enables me to confront the enemy's attacks against me. It equips me with hope to share with the lost and comfort for the hurting.

I never knew that paying close attention to God's Word when the Bible was in front of me would help me meditate on His truth when there was no Bible around. It clears out the poisonous residue of my toxic thinking and replaces it with the joy of close companionship with Jesus. As truth finds a home in my mind, God's Word is readily available when I need Him most. This can be true for you too.

Today is the day to start. Identify lies, renounce and replace them with truth, and savor the freedom Christ died to give you. *Today* is the day. No turning back.

TRAVELING TOGETHER

Spend some time talking with God or discussing the following with an accountability partner or small group.

▸ In this chapter, we observed that what you think about God is the most important thing about you. Knowing His truth sets you free. Look up the following verses and deliberately decide to bring these truths about who God is to mind throughout the week.

- He knows you (Isa. 43:1).
- He sings over you (Zeph. 3:17).
- He upholds you (Isa. 41:10).
- He cares about you (1 Pet. 5:7).
- He watches over you (Gen. 28:15).
- He guides you (Luke 1:79).
- He never leaves you (Matt. 28:20).

▸ Identify a lie you regularly believe and actively replace it with truth. For instance, if you've struggled with the lie that you're worthless, apply a truth like Isaiah 43:4 to your life: "You are precious in my eyes, and honored, and I love you."

▸ Is God's Word currently at home in your heart and mind? Why or why not?

▸ How do you respond to God's truth in Isaiah 26:3–4? "You keep him in perfect peace whose mind is stayed on you, because he trusts in you. Trust in the LORD forever, for the LORD GOD is an everlasting rock."

▸ Make Romans 12:2 a prayer, asking God to transform you into a new person by changing how you think.

POINTS TO PONDER AS YOU PROGRESS

God never uses words to condemn His children:
loser, failure, no good, useless, stupid.

God calls His children *Beloved, Redeemed,
Chosen, Disciples, Heirs.*

The names God calls you are the only ones that
matter. If what you hear isn't what God has spoken,
stop and reconsider. Examine your thoughts in
the light of God's thoughts toward you.

From Your Plan
to God's Purpose

IN THE UNITED STATES ARMY, nothing is random. *Nothing.* After nine years of service, I can assure you: from how beds are made to how a rescue mission is conducted, purpose and precision mark every dynamic of a soldier's life. Before the Army commissioned me as an officer, I sneered at the idea of shining my shoes. It seemed so pointless. But even that activity, I discovered, was done for a specific and important reason: respect begins with an appearance indicative of complete situational awareness.

In my Army platoon, we worked out for the first 10 percent of our day. The purpose here? Not simply so we could look good but because exercise starts the engines of our bodies, infusing us with energy and momentum for the other 90 percent of our day. Eating and sleeping also had specific purposes. For an Army serviceperson, food is the fuel that powers body and mind. In the military, sleep isn't taken for granted. Every good soldier knows that being sleep-deprived is a lot like drunkenness. No one wants to serve alongside a platoon mate who stayed up until three in the morning playing video games. The purpose of sleep is to keep the body and mind at peak performance.

With great resolve and purpose, my platoon completed dangerous and massive tasks like transferring ammunition and explosives in Humvees. We also directed that same focus and attention to what civilians might view as "small things." Purpose reminded me, and all Army men and women, that airing up the tire of a van can be a life-and-death situation for those driving that vehicle into enemy territory. Nothing is half-done, half-baked, or arbitrary in the US Army.

Military bases simplify life for servicepeople. Every essential service is readily available and easily accessible on a military installation: grocery stores, medical facilities, police and fire departments, shopping outlets, transportation amenities, hair salons and barber shops, even entertainment options like bowling alleys and/or movie theaters. Is there purpose in this too? Absolutely! Staying on base as much as possible serves the purpose of keeping our minds disciplined and under control.

Establishing and maintaining healthy relationships also fit the unifying purpose of the Army. When you have a battle buddy in your platoon—a person you know you'll have to eat, sleep, train, and serve alongside for the next two or three years—it has a way of making you want to work out any kinks in your relationship. Keeping relationships out of the toxic zone might save your life one day! Senseless disagreements and petty squabbling don't fit with the purpose of a soldier's life. My Army days taught me the incomparable value of good friends who've "been through it" with you.

I learned other lessons as well, such as the purpose of submitting wants to genuine needs and the purpose of respecting those who've gone before; seasoned soldiers regularly saved me from making major mistakes as a young serviceman. In the Army, gray hair is often worn on a head of honor. For lifelong soldiers, getting older usually means great experience and ever-increasing regard for the singular focus and purpose of military life.

Military service is difficult, demanding, and dangerous; it can also be incredibly fulfilling. For some people, it provides direction for a life swerving off course. For others, the intense resolve and purposefulness of a soldier's life are merely an extension of their natural internal drive and single-mindedness, a characteristic of the best military servicepeople.

I wonder what the church would look like if every Christian understood and committed to their God-given purpose as good soldiers submit to the US Army's aims? I wonder what life would be like if I had learned, much earlier, that my plans pale in comparison to the glorious purposes of

Jehovah Sabaoth, "the God of Angel Armies"? What if we, as followers of Jesus Christ, did nothing half-baked or at random but knew and lived out our purpose every day? I wonder . . .

WHERE WE'VE COME FROM

During my Army years, purpose formed my plans. No one asked me what I wanted to do, told me to follow my heart, or invited me to look within to determine my next steps. Everything was laid out before me. And it all made sense.

In the world outside the military installation . . . not so much.

I watched as a friend, Kathe, got into a physically abusive relationship with a viciously manipulative guy she met in college. Traumatized by the experience, bearing an intense weight of pain and shame, Kathe tried to self-medicate with drugs, hookups, and alcohol. As her escapes morphed into addictions, my friend spiraled into serious PTSD and landed in rehab.

Kathe's parents, devout believers, had raised her in faith. They connected her with a Christ-following counselor who helped her sort through the past and look toward the future. Kathe promised her friends and accountability partners she'd stay clean. Eventually, when it seemed Kathe was on solid emotional ground, she stopped counseling.

Next thing we all knew, Kathe was leaving Oklahoma with a one-way ticket to travel the world. Apparently, she'd been watching influencer videos from travel gurus lounging on beaches and touting the beauty of self-discovery. Kathe flew off to find herself.

I'm not going to lie; on social media, her life looked like a dazzling dream. Followers, friends, and family praised her steps toward self-love. Kathe spoke of the freedom of "living her truth."

Then she started connecting with a different guy in every new country, someone who seemed part tour guide and part source of security. It became harder to witness the life Kathe was choosing.

The reality was, whether she was in Oklahoma or Okinawa, Kathe's truth was still rooted in trauma and pain. She wasn't discovering herself but rather running away from self-destruction. Her path looked good—even amazing—in snapshots on social media, but the deeper truths of insecurity, lack of purpose, and confusion became evident as time went on.

Out of money, Kathe flew home, settled in the US, and discovered not "herself" but her unplanned pregnancy. There was nowhere left to run, no money to finance another escape. Afraid of what her devoutly Christian family would say, Kathe felt more alone than ever before.

Instead of being rejected by her Christ-following family and friends, though, Kathe found an incredible support system for raising her beloved son. It took becoming unexpectedly pregnant for the reality to set in: Kathe's plans for her life—the supposed freedom of living her own truth and the beauty of looking within—had left her emptier and more confused than ever. She chased happiness and surrendered purpose. She ran after self-love and found heartache.

There are a whole lot of Kathes out there. Do you see some of yourself in her story? I sure do. My long, winding, and rocky road toward Jesus included a lot of looking within, living "my truth," and trying to make and work my plans. All of it went nowhere.

Like Kathe, who didn't know who she was without an adventure, a guy, or an Insta-worthy photo, I didn't know who I was without accomplishments, accolades, and applause. I believed my purpose was to succeed. Power was key to that, so I pursued it at all costs. My identity was wrapped up in what I did, how I did it, and the results I achieved.

I opened this chapter by highlighting the incredible focus of Army life because I wanted to contrast the purposefulness of a soldier's existence with the daily confusion and searching many of us have experienced. You may not have literally wandered the world like Kathe, but you might be wandering the web trying to find yourself. You may not have looked within but rather to person after person (parents? profs? partners?) to give you a sense of self. This is what it's like to search for identity, to search for purpose.

This is the way of the dragon.

If you boil things down, life presents us with two ultimate paths: the way of the dragon or the way of the Lamb.[1] True, we may meander a bit on roads that seem to go elsewhere, but all paths eventually flow into either the stream of self or the stream of surrender.

My upbringing, intensity, and talent aligned with the way of the dragon. My whole life I had been groomed to desire and acquire power. It started in my career as an elite athlete. Whether I was playing football and basketball or running track, the teams I was on didn't lose much; this all heightened my desire for power and accolades. I equated winning with a strong work ethic; if I put in the hard work, I would win, and—of course—winning was both the goal and the only acceptable outcome. Sports weren't about teamwork for me; I was there to make success happen. My life purpose entwined with work, winning, and worldliness.

During my military service, the way of the dragon infected me further. I went in as a commissioned Army officer; others who had enlisted and served honorably, some for decades, would salute me. That was intoxicating in the worst possible way. I began to obsess over how many ranks I could climb, how many more people I could get to salute me. I was desperate to achieve and desperate for praise; my heart and purposes were entirely bent toward self.

Walking this path led me to books like *The 48 Laws of Power*, *The Secret*, and *The Power of Now*. The big (though false) lessons I took away: my consciousness could exert power over every aspect of my life; if I went after something hard enough, I could accomplish or acquire it; if I looked inside long enough, I'd find myself. Manifestation declarations became my mantras.

This bubble of self-determination burst when I realized that all of this came down to one thing: me. These ideas were as frail as I was inside, despite my best efforts to conceal any and every weakness. Yeah, I may have been winning or making rank or smiling my way through life, but I knew deep down that if it all came down to me and "the universe," I was in big trouble.

I don't know where you are on the journey, but all of us begin the journey of life on the way of the dragon. You can confirm this by watching any group of toddlers. No one has to teach them to say "No" or "Mine." Selfishness comes standard in every human heart. Submission and surrender don't.

Surrender isn't a popular word; it's hated almost as much as the word *submission*. It implies losing, and we can agree that no one wakes up in the morning saying, "I'm ready to lose today." We live in a competitive culture where if you ain't winnin', you sinnin'! But there's a greater purpose to which we're called: submission is success, obeying is over-coming, and yielding is climbing in the kingdom of God. That's where we're headed.

The truth about who we are doesn't live in our hearts but in God's heart, which is revealed in His Word. Our plans and God's purposes aren't always mutually exclusive; I'm grateful for that! I'll tell you what, though; our plans and the purpose of God can either conflict or coalesce, depending on which path we choose.

WHERE WE'RE HEADED

I've described the way of the dragon and how it impacts our sense of purpose and identity. This is the stream of self. What of the other stream, the stream of surrender? How does the way of the Lamb differ, and where does it lead?

On the simplest level, it's the way of Jesus. Or rather, Jesus *is* the Way (see John 14:6).

The way of the Lamb involves a willingness and faith-fulness to grow in Christlikeness. It includes, as Matthew 16:24 identifies, a commitment to deny our self and take up our cross, not in some randomly sadistic way but with laser-focused purpose.

> For whoever would save his life will lose it, but whoever loses his life for my sake will find it. For what will it profit a man if he gains the whole world and forfeits his soul? Or what shall a man give in return for his soul? (vv. 25–26)

God wants your life—all of it. There are a whole lot of ce-lebs, pro athletes, and social media influencers who look like they've "gained the whole world." I only wonder how many of them have forfeited their souls in the process. Thank God it's not up to me to figure that out. I stand before God accountable for one person: myself. And I don't want to forfeit my soul.

That's why I choose the way of the Lamb each and every day.

The first time I said yes to Christ, I was a hotheaded, sixteen-year-old punk, too talented for my own good. I'd just finished football practice and sat in the locker room with my teammates, listening to a visiting coach who came to encourage us. Turns out he was part of a group called FCA (Fellowship of Christian Athletes). This dude brought it. His message was upbeat, and I was hooked.

I went up after the talk ended and asked if he could tell me more about this Jesus life. He said, "Rashawn, God has a wonderful plan for your life, and you can have that starting today." Who wouldn't want that?

For the next eight months, I was super involved in FCA. And for a long time, the whole promise of abundant life seemed realistic. Then stuff started happening. Bad stuff.

A teammate's mom, a devoted follower of Christ, was diagnosed with cancer and died shortly thereafter. A Christian classmate, a really cool girl, was killed in a senseless car crash. I lost my job and started to question God. *If You love Your people, Jesus, why does all this happen? Is this the abundant life You promised me?* It was wonderful, all right—as in, I *wondered* if this was the fullness I'd signed up to receive.

And so I got confused about the way of the Lamb. It wasn't that visiting coach's fault, but the message "God has a wonderful plan for your life" got twisted in my mind. I heard it as "God will give you the wonderful life you have planned for yourself." When that didn't happen, I slowly but steadily began turning back to my old ways.

I want to be super clear with you: the way of the Lamb is the road to everlasting joy. Like the psalmist, I can confirm of God: "You make known to me the path of life; in your presence there is fullness of joy; at your right hand are pleasures forevermore" (16:11). The way of the Lamb is also the path of peace. In heaven, Jesus "will wipe away every tear . . . and death shall be no more, neither shall there be mourning, nor crying, nor pain anymore, for the former things have passed away" (Rev. 21:4).

Hallelujah and amen! We can celebrate this today and always, giving thanks to God.

Let me be super clear with you about this too: the way of the Lamb is also the way of complete surrender. Jesus Christ did not come to earth to confirm my wonderful plans for life but to end them. Like the apostle Paul, "I have been crucified with Christ. It is no longer I who live, but Christ who lives in me. And the life I now live in the flesh I live by faith in the Son of God, who loved me and gave himself for me" (Gal. 2:20).

God's purpose for my life is sanctification; 1 Thessalonians 4:3 makes this supremely evident. His purpose for your life is sanctification too. What we go through we grow through. There's a purpose behind all our problems. That purpose isn't always to comfort us (make us feel better) but to conform us (make us like Christ). And we don't become more like Jesus—which is what *sanctification* means—without taking up our cross. That's why the apostle Peter urges,

> Beloved, do not be surprised at the fiery trial when it comes upon you to test you, as though something strange were happening to you. But rejoice insofar as you share Christ's sufferings, that you may also rejoice and be glad when his glory is revealed. (1 Pet. 4:12–13)

The way of the Lamb is the path of abundant life. "Surely goodness and mercy shall follow me all the days of my life, and I shall dwell in the house of the LORD forever," Psalm 23:6 promises. We're headed to eternal fulfillment.

The way of the Lamb is also a path of suffering. God promises that even our pain will be used for His glory, though. Romans 8:28 affirms, "For those who love God all things work together for good, for those who are called according to his purpose." As has often been said but still bears repeating, this verse does *not* claim all things are good. Some things—teenagers in fatal car accidents, mamas dying from cancer, job loss, pandemics, and racism—are *not* good. Can the Almighty God use these bad things for His purposes, though? I thank God that He can *and does*. And that's what enables us to continue on the way of the Lamb, fulfilling God's purpose for our lives.

I don't want you to journey with Jesus thinking abundant life equals an easy life, like I did. I don't want you to even consider following the way of the dragon, let alone walk a destructive path like mine. The way of the Lamb isn't always wonderful, but it's always worth it. If that's where you want to head—maybe that's where you're already faithfully heading!—let's look at ways to walk free and unhindered on the way of the Lamb.

TRAVELING LIGHTLY

Jesus once told His disciples a parable about planting seed in different types of ground. According to Luke 8,

> Now the parable is this: The seed is the word of God. . . . The ones on the rock are those who, when they hear the word, receive it with joy. But these have no root; they believe for a while, and in time of testing fall away. (vv. 11, 13)

Based on what I've shared in this book, maybe you recognize my younger self in this parable? During my teens, the seed of Christ's truth fell on the rocky road of my heart.

I welcomed the message initially but fell away when trials came and doubts arose. No one warned me that my character would be tested—and character building is a slow process. I chose to give up instead of grow up.

Later, during my early adulthood, my heart mirrored another part of Jesus's story: "And as for what [seed] fell among the thorns, they are those who hear, but as they go on their way they are choked by the cares and riches and pleasures of life, and their fruit does not mature" (v. 14). You can probably guess that traveling the way of the dragon is a "cares, riches, and pleasures of the world" kind of path. When I worked in the Los Angeles music and influencer scene, this described me perfectly. My worldly lifestyle choked the Word of God right out of my life.

Mercifully, God drew me back to Himself. He invaded my life with light and love in my darkest moment, when I literally had a gun stuffed in my mouth. I told that story in my first book, *Start Where You Are*, and I encourage you to read it if you've ever faced depression so deep you thought you couldn't endure one more day. Through a radical conversion experience that included a forgotten Bible discovered in a suitcase under my bed, a social media post from a Christian girl I'd met once upon a time, and several other only-God-could-have-done-that circumstances, I committed to the way of the Lamb in total surrender. It was God's purpose or nothing. This time there would be no turning back.

What I quickly discovered, however, was that I was traveling Christ's way with a lot of dragon's way baggage. Maybe you've sensed this on your journey with Jesus? You want to follow wholeheartedly, but you keep getting drawn back to your old ways? I've definitely been there. Every day I'm fighting the good fight of faith. And through the ups and downs of my faith adventure, I've discovered that to travel lightly on the way of the Lamb, I have to joyfully cast off every purpose that's not aligned with God's. Similar to my Army self, I have to maintain laser focus on who I am and what I'm called to do in Christ.

I was created—and so were you—to know God and make Him known. That is our ultimate purpose in life. And as I hope you remember from chapter 1, your identity is found in Christ too. He is, all at once, your way, your truth, and your life (see John 14:6). Jesus gives us purpose, identity, and direction. In John 8:12, He proclaims, "I am the light of the world. Whoever follows me will not walk in darkness, but will have the light of life."

With these words, our Lord reveals that darkness is a choice. Light is available to us on the way of the Lamb. Why would we choose darkness?

You and I need to allow God to light the flame of our hearts, give us power to push back on any darkness, and enable us to shed any way-of-the-dragon baggage we might be carrying. For me, this included setting aside my desire to be applauded, influential, and successful in the world's eyes. The way of the Lamb is the path of humility, which—let's just say—isn't super popular with the dragon.

After I received Jesus as the priceless treasure of my heart, the lure of the dragon's ways tempted me to either rely on the warm praises of other Christians or focus on their cold criticism of me. I got caught up in having a seat at the table with influential kingdom leaders at huge conferences. I allowed teachers who weren't doctrinally sound to infect my thinking. Don't allow the enemy to tempt you toward the dead end of the "name it and claim it" message. Instead, choose the path of promise and train your mind to stay on the track of truth, which is the way of the Lamb: this always leads to prayer (intimacy with Christ) and obedience (imitating the ways of Christ).

I was tempted by some of the dragon's ways as the health and wealth "prosperity gospel" (remember, this has nothing to do with the *real* gospel of Christ) encouraged me to make God an accessory, not my whole outfit. I became distracted from my purpose in Jesus. I had to confess and cast all this off, and if you've ever felt tempted in these ways, I urge you to cast them off too. "Let us also lay aside every weight," the writer of Hebrews commands us, "and sin which clings so closely, and let us run with endurance the race that is set before us, looking to Jesus, the founder and perfecter of our faith" (12:1–2). This alone aligns with our true purpose: knowing God, being known by Him, and making Him known.

To close out this chapter, let's look at how, once we've determined to travel lightly on the way of the Lamb, we can do so with wisdom and strength.

TRAVELING WISELY

In 2 Timothy 2:4, the apostle Paul invites us to consider that "no soldier gets entangled in civilian pursuits, since his aim is to please the one who enlisted him." Soldiers confidently and precisely pursue their purpose. The application is simple: to be like Jesus, we should live in the same manner.

Think of the difference between a cruise ship and an aircraft carrier. A cruise ship is all about pleasure—there is as much food as you want, the alcohol flows, endless forms of entertainment are available, and every day is arranged around you. Do you know how many people come home from cruises five or ten pounds heavier, sick, and more dissatisfied with their lives than when they left?

By contrast, on an aircraft carrier there's one purpose: to complete the mission, whatever it takes. Though there may be many difficulties along the way, completing the mission is both fulfilling and life affirming.

Do you think God created your life to be more like a pleasure cruise or a precise mission?

I'll make this short and sweet: God wants you to live on purpose, for a purpose. This is the way of wisdom, and I never want you to turn back.

TRAVELING TOGETHER

Spend some time talking with God or discussing the following with an accountability partner or small group.

- ▸ What way-of-the-dragon baggage might God be calling you to cast off today?
- ▸ Read Luke 11:43 and Matthew 20:16. The Pharisees were highly religious people who didn't have an authentic relationship with God. What do these verses

teach us about their (and our?) desire to have influence, look out for number one, and be part of the "right" circles?

▸ Do you agree or disagree that some people fall away from the faith because of false gospels that feed into our desires for comfort, protection, and ease?

▸ The way of the Lamb includes surrender and suffering. Use the words of 1 Peter 5:10 to jump-start a prayer of gratitude: "And after you have suffered a little while, the God of all grace, who has called you to his eternal glory in Christ, will himself restore, confirm, strengthen, and establish you."

POINTS TO PONDER AS YOU PROGRESS

Instead of praying, "Lord, *cover* my plans," ask God to *uncover* His purposes for your life. His wisdom, power, and presence always exceed our projections. His projects outstretch ours. His perspectives are wider. His purpose is deeper. His plan is greater.

From Being Spilled Empty to Being Filled with Plenty

The only people who truly embrace the word of God are those who have first been deeply embraced by the Spirit of God.

DENISSE COPELAND

WHEN I WAS GROWING UP, Oklahoma Sooner football dominated many of my thoughts. I dreamed of putting on that crimson and cream jersey and exiting the tunnel at Owen Field, blinking in the sunlight as thousands of Sooner fans screamed us toward victory. *Boomer . . . Sooners!!!*

A fan in the truest sense of the word, I began planning early on how and when I could get recruited by OU. It seemed the easiest route would involve moving from Florida to Oklahoma, establishing residency, and applying for

"in-state" admission. So I did what any incoming sopho-
more in high school full of his own plans and dreams would
do and asked my dad if I could move to Oklahoma. I had
an aunt and cousins who lived there, and fortunately they
agreed to take me in. Though I still sometimes can't believe
it, my parents said yes and off I went. *Let's go!*

The first month was like a dream. I was on my way; I
loved going to school with my cousins; everything was new
and exciting. As the days flew by and the weeks added up
to months, though, I started to experience a sadness I just
couldn't shake.

I know many of you did not grow up with healthy relationships with your parents. I grieve with you over that. God
gave me strong bonds with my folks, though, and I missed
them terribly when I lived in Oklahoma.

Since my aunt wasn't married and my cousins' dad was
not part of their everyday lives, I had no father figure in
Oklahoma. It honestly surprised me how much I missed
that. Being apart from my dad helped me realize what his
steadying, guiding presence provided for me. I noticed a
sense of recklessness and rebelliousness cropping up in me,
and though I wasn't a believer at the time, I knew these
feelings weren't leading me anywhere good. If I'd been at
home, Dad would have given me a stern talking-to about
some of my ways. I might have rolled my eyes (only after he
left the room, of course) at his protectiveness, but when the
security of my father's presence and his solid advice were
no longer readily available, I truly missed them. The truth
is, at that point my dad was the only "ever-present help in
trouble" (Ps. 46:1 NIV) I knew.

I also missed his love. It was a love I never had to question. Fifteen-year-old guys—particularly focused athletes like I was—aren't really "supposed" to talk about missing their dad's love. What? *Whatever.* I totally missed the words, "Son, I love you," which my dad often said, and the bear hugs he'd freely give. Because this was 2003, before technology brought humanity video chatting and social media, I had to rely on written texts, scattered phone calls, and snail-mail letters (yes, some of us actually remember sending and receiving things other than ads and bills via our mailboxes).

By the time I flew back to Florida for Christmas break, I literally ached to be at home with my father. When I deplaned in Miami and Dad put his arms around me, I actually cried.

It's been said that "absence makes the heart grow fonder" and "you don't really know what you have until it's gone." Both of these proved true as I missed my dad. But as I reflect back on this season of life, I also realize God was teaching me an even deeper truth, a truth I wouldn't fully understand until years later, when I began walking more closely with Jesus.

It's one thing to be *told* that you are loved. That's a gift. It's an even greater treasure to *know* that you are loved. But guess what! It's the greatest gift of all to *experience* love, to be caught up in the warm embrace of a papa who loves you, who puts your head against his chest and affirms, "I love you." Experiencing love empowers us; it changes things. It changes everything.

As I look back on my fifteen-year-old self, I see a young man being taught by God that the Holy Spirit's presence—His power to testify to my heart that I am loved and protected, His guidance, and His protection—is not a nice add-on to life but *life itself*. One of the Holy Spirit's primary roles is to reveal the love and truth of God to us, in a similar—though far more glorious—manner to how separation from my dad revealed the treasure of his love to me. The Holy Spirit's love and power far surpass my father's, though God used my good relationship with my dad and that season of separation to teach me about His Spirit's role in my life.

If you currently feel, or have ever felt, a sense of emptiness or lostness, a sense of sadness over something missing, I invite you to journey with me as we look at the role of God the Holy Spirit in our life journey. Romans 8:6 tells us that "to set the mind on the flesh is death, but to set the mind on the Spirit is life and peace." Being close with the Spirit is not simply a good idea; it's a life-and-death proposition. Let's not miss out on anything He's got in store for us.

WHERE WE'VE COME FROM

As we've journeyed together through this book, we've looked at some pretty heavy things: our dirty desires, our toxic thinking, the broken ways we identify ourselves. We've also seen how Jesus takes us from these dark places and into His light and life. Some of you, however, may have a difficult time grasping God's love for you when you consider how bleak or depraved your life has been. I deeply understand this struggle. I've been there.

When I began to journey with Jesus, I knew God's mercy covered all my sin. However, I only began to *experience* Christ's grace—to feel it, savor it, and see it flow out of me to others—in new ways when I drew closer to the Holy Spirit.

Being filled with the Spirit of God means walking in the light, being swept up in the river of God's mercy that flows from the cross, from His heavenly throne, from Christ's heart to mine, and from mine into others. When we allow the Spirit to fill us, His love and grace flow right back out, building up the church, blessing others. If we are filled with God's Spirit, mercy will flow everywhere we go.

No matter where you've been thus far in your walk with Christ, I want you to experience more of the benefits of intimate closeness with God the Holy Spirit. Embracing the fullness of our great God changes us, especially when we're struggling. I've found some of the sweetest and strongest blessings of God the Spirit when times of trouble and darkness threaten me.

You may be familiar with the verse in the Psalms that promises, "Even though I walk through the valley of the shadow of death, I will fear no evil, for you are with me; your rod and your staff, they comfort me" (23:4). The Hebrew phrase translated here as "valley of the shadow of death" can be understood as deep darkness. Think of the kind of darkness that suffocates and terrifies you more with every step, the kind of darkness that screams at you.

King David, who wrote Psalm 23, did *not* turn back because he was convinced of God's goodness and mercy (see v. 6). The only way David could face deep darkness was because he knew the Almighty in whom he could rest and under whose wings he could hide (see Ps. 91). Shadows exist because light does. In fact, darkness is best described as the absence of light. Because God, the Light of the World, has come, we don't have to walk in darkness any longer. And because God's Spirit dwells in every believer, we can experience the fullness of God every moment of every day. Christians are not a spilled-empty people but rather a filled-with-plenty family. Fullness—of mercy, comfort, truth, and life—is the Spirit's gift to us.

At this point you may be thinking, *Wouldn't everyone want this?* Yes, I imagine they do. Some powerful and damaging misconceptions about the Holy Spirit have permeated our church culture, however, and kept people from experiencing the help of God's Spirit, available to all believers. Because some of us have felt confused or even leery of embracing the work of the Holy Spirit based on what we have or haven't been taught, I'd like to offer you an introduction to His character, as revealed by His Word.

Before we start, I want to acknowledge that the infinite majesty of God—Father, Son, and Spirit—can never be described in full by any human, let alone me. "Who can fathom the Spirit of the LORD," the prophet Isaiah asks, "or instruct the LORD as his counselor?" (40:13 NIV). The obvious answer here is *no one.* No one can perfectly understand the all-powerful, all-knowing, eternal God in all of His glory. Does that mean we shouldn't even try to comprehend Him or help others do so? As the apostle Paul might say, "By no means!" We are called to press into deeper knowledge of and love for God in the midst of our human limitations.

In fact, one of the Holy Spirit's primary roles is to lead us in truth (see John 16:13), so though I tremble in awe of God and grasp the immensity of the challenge of describing His ways and work, I also rejoice to learn and share truth.

The Holy Spirit is part of the triune God, the third member of the Trinity. God the Holy Spirit is not separate from God, our Father, or from Jesus, our Savior. When we use the phrase "God's Spirit," we are not talking about a separate part of God but His incomparable, divine fullness.

The Holy Spirit is a person, not an "it," a thing, or an impersonal force. As Paul closed his second letter to the believers at Corinth, he prayed this benediction: "The grace of the Lord Jesus Christ and the love of God and the fellowship of the Holy Spirit be with you all" (2 Cor. 13:14). The Holy Spirit is not something but *someone* with whom we fellowship. We are called to a relationship with God, so when I speak of being empowered or filled by the Holy Spirit, please think of this in a relationship context. We must never treat God's Spirit as a force we can use to get what we want or even to display God's power in miraculous ways. The fullness of the Spirit in our lives is always for the glory of God and the building up of His children, brought together and united in His church.

God the Holy Spirit comes to dwell in us the moment we receive Christ as our treasure (see John 14:17). What an awesome and humbling thought . . . God *in* me. In *you*. Wow! Romans 8:1–17 highlights this truth. "The Spirit himself bears witness with our spirit that we are children of God, and if children, then heirs—heirs of God and fellow heirs with Christ, provided we suffer with him in order that we may also be glorified with him" (vv. 16–17). Ephesians 1:13–14 furthers this point: "In him you also, when you heard the word of truth, the gospel of your salvation, and believed in him, were sealed with the promised Holy Spirit, who is the guarantee of our inheritance until we acquire possession of it, to the praise of his glory." To sum up, God the Holy Spirit dwells in you, internally assures you of God's love, and seals you with every promise of God for all eternity. Breathtaking, isn't it?

Because the Spirit dwells in us, Jesus even told His disciples that it was to their advantage that He return to glory and send His Spirit (see John 16:7). I imagine it must have been difficult for Christ's followers to understand this. Even I, two thousand years later, sometimes have a tough time fathoming how anything could be better than having the living, breathing Jesus right by my side. But then reality hits me: Jesus *is* right by me. Better yet, He's right *in me* as the Holy Spirit. He's in you too, if you've confessed Him as Lord.

Instead of our hearts being filled with sorrow that Jesus is no longer physically on earth with us, we are filled with joy and sealed with a closeness, a dearer and deeper friendship, a fullness that could only happen by His coming *into* us. Jesus's body may no longer be with us, but His heart never left. This is the grand benefit our Lord spoke of when He promised another Helper would come, giving us not just a head knowledge of Jesus's words but a heart knowledge that sears the truth and love of God *into* us.

When He walked on earth, Jesus told and showed His disciples that He loved them (see John 13 for a beautiful example of this). I'm sure some of them really believed Him.

The Bible also tells us, however, that after Jesus was crucified, resurrected, and returned to glory, God the Holy Spirit came in a way none of them had previously experienced. Acts 2 records the tale, and it's a wild one. Let's turn there as we look forward to where we're going as we walk in step with God the Holy Spirit.

WHERE WE'RE HEADED

On the day of Pentecost, the Bible tells us Jesus's disciples

> were all together in one place. And suddenly there came from heaven a sound like a mighty rushing wind, and it filled the entire house where they were sitting. And divided tongues as of fire appeared to them and rested on each one of them. And they were all filled with the Holy Spirit and began to speak in other tongues as the Spirit gave them utterance. (Acts 2:1–4)

A massive crowd gathered, and Peter—emboldened and empowered—preached the gospel message: "Repent and be baptized every one of you in the name of Jesus Christ for the forgiveness of your sins, and you will receive the gift of the Holy Spirit" (v. 38). Thousands received the gift of salvation and the sealing of the Spirit that day.

It absolutely blows my mind that the same Holy Spirit who filled the room at Pentecost is the same Spirit ready to fill us every day. The same Spirit who raised Christ from the dead is within us. He gives us determination and perseverance, even in the midst of adversity and danger. He fills us with plenty no matter how empty our pasts have left us. That's great news!

God the Holy Spirit is a priceless gift. To receive this gift, we need only believe and receive. Unfortunately, many believers acknowledge God the Spirit but never treasure and cherish Him. As a result, these people live with little power and little hope. May this not be true of me or you!

God dwelling within you can—and should—change everything about your life. And that's a good thing. If the Holy Spirit of God within you comes with the same power that set fire to the early church, don't you think your life should look different from that of your nonbelieving neighbor, coworker, or family member? It should . . . big time. And the way our lives look different is through the power of God the Spirit.

According to Romans 8:13, "If you live according to the flesh you will die, but if by the Spirit you put to death the deeds of the body, you will live." God's Spirit empowers us to kill sin and live holy lives. We can white-knuckle our way to a certain amount of moral goodness, but living a Christ-like life is flat-out impossible without the empowering of God's Spirit within us. He makes us more like Jesus as we walk in step with Him.

Later in Romans 8, we also discover that the Holy Spirit prays through us, especially when we don't know what to say or how to say it. This gives me so much comfort. I just don't always have the right words. The "Spirit helps us in our weakness. For we do not know what to pray for as we ought, but the Spirit himself intercedes for us with groanings too deep for words" (v. 26). What a precious promise! "The Spirit intercedes for the saints according to the will of God" (v. 27). Talk about priceless gifts . . . God prays in us, helping us in our weakness.

Before you received Jesus as your Lord and Savior, you were continually emptied by running after things that drained and destroyed you. The prophet Jeremiah records God's words to those living apart from Him: "They have forsaken me, the fountain of living waters, and hewed out cisterns for themselves, broken cisterns that can hold no water" (Jer. 2:13).

You were spilled empty before Christ, but—because of the gift of the Spirit—now you can live filled with plenty. To do that, however, you've got to shed some baggage.

TRAVELING LIGHTLY

The Bible tells us we can walk with the Spirit in one of two ways: we can grieve Him or we can bear fruit through Him (see Eph. 4:30; Gal. 5:22–25). Put as simply as that, I'm betting most of you would choose to bear fruit. The trouble is, a whole lot of us are grieving the Spirit as we journey through life.

We can grieve God's Spirit through sin, as Ephesians 4:30–31 teaches: "And do not grieve the Holy Spirit of God, by whom you were sealed for the day of redemption. Let all bitterness and wrath and anger and clamor and slander be put away from you, along with all malice." When we're raging or gossipy, resentful or harsh, we actually hurt the Holy Spirit. What a horrible thought.

The message of turning away from sin is one we don't hear too often in today's world. Even churches sometimes fear offending people, losing congregants, or souring their biggest donors if there's too much talk about sin. But we *must* expose the kingdom of darkness so that God's kingdom can come and His will be done. Sin is the very reason so many of us have been messy, wayward, and wandering; sin grieves the Holy Spirit.

I'm so grateful His mercies are tender and that He's constantly calling us out of the ugly grip of sin. By the power of God's Spirit, we don't have to live enslaved by the thoughts or patterns in which we used to walk. We can shed that baggage. We don't have to grieve the Holy Spirit; He's here to help us, not hurt us. Let's welcome His help, not reject it. Without the constant help the Holy Spirit provides, sin will wrap around us like an anaconda with a death grip, leaving us lifeless—an empty shell. Don't fret yet! Praise be to God who sent Jesus to destroy the work of Satan (see 1 John 3:8).

God, so rich in mercy, fills us to overflowing (see Ps. 23:5). He does not withhold His mercy from any of us, no matter how "great" a sinner we might be. In fact, His very heart longs for those who are far off, for those sinners who have rejected Him. God the Holy Spirit highlights this mercy, reminding us that we can overcome our sin, even our darkest of sins, in Jesus. Though our sin grieves God's heart, our repentance delights Him (see Luke 15:7).

Neglect and disbelief can also grieve God's Spirit. First Thessalonians 5:19–22 unpacks this: "Do not quench the Spirit. Do not despise prophecies, but test everything; hold fast to what is good. Abstain from every form of evil." It's startling to realize that people can become so caught up in fearing "emotional excess" or being "overly spiritual" that they can quench the fire of the Spirit.

As Francis Chan so wisely puts in his book on the Holy Spirit, *The Forgotten God*,

> Given our talent set, experience, and education, many of us are fairly capable of living rather successfully (according to the world's standards) without any strength from the Holy Spirit. . . . Even our church growth can happen without Him. Let's be honest: If you combine a charismatic speaker, a talented worship band, and some hip, creative events, people will attend your church. Yet this does not mean the Holy Spirit of God is actively working and moving in the lives of the people who are coming.[1]

Brothers and sisters, this cannot continue. I don't want us to squander the fullness available to us. We've got to get rid of the baggage of self-assurance, independence, and self-direction so rampant in the American church (and in our own hearts). We're called, instead, to live in humility, utter dependence, and total reliance on God's Spirit.

This is not a super popular calling, however. People would much rather hear that the Spirit will empower them to live their best life now; that the Spirit wants them to be healthy, wealthy, and wise; and that He can and will do whatever they want if they have enough faith. Faith in what? In a god they can control? In a force that's more like the one Rey or Luke Skywalker harnesses in *Star Wars*? That's not who our Lord is.

He is the Almighty God, a consuming fire, the Holy One who was and is and is to come (see Heb. 12:29; Rev. 1:8). I don't need more of me; I need less of me and more of Him. That's the real secret: His power is perfected in my weakness (see John 3:30; 2 Cor. 12:10). In the past, I was emptied by sin; now I'm filled to overflowing by the Spirit of God within me. This is true of every Christian. If we believe or live in less, we quench the Spirit of God.

While we're not called to welcome every expression of faith we see as the work or word of God, looking back at the verses we read in 1 Thessalonians 5 reminds us that we are called to test and hold fast to what is good and true. In other words, savor the meat and spit out the bones. We grieve the Holy Spirit when we neglect His work and quench His power, whether it be through sin, fear, or carelessness. These are things we need to shed to travel well. There are also things we can do to walk more closely with God the Spirit. Let's shift our attention to those things now.

TRAVELING WISELY

The precious and pleasing Spirit of Christ takes me from reading the Bible and reading about the love of God to really experiencing it, not just as a doctrine but as a present reality. The Holy Spirit magnifies what Christ has done, shining a bright, blinding light on how real the love of Jesus is for me. The Holy Spirit moves me from hearing about His love to seeing His love, from seeing His love to feeling His love, from feeling His love to truly enjoying His love.

This continual movement toward closeness goes beyond knowing what God has done; I love Him *for who He is* as the Spirit moves in me. This makes a daily difference as I journey through life. This is the power that fills and equips me. This is your birthright too, as a follower of Jesus.

God the Holy Spirit continues (with seamless glory) the work begun by Christ when He walked on earth (see John 14:16–17). God's Spirit stirs our affections and leaves us in awe of our Savior. Has it been a while since your heart was stirred? If so, stop right now and pray that the Holy Spirit would allow you to feel the heart of Christ deeply and powerfully.

The Holy Spirit enables us to know and overflow with Christ's love in a compelling, personal way, the way the apostle Paul identifies in Galatians 2:20: "I live by faith in the Son of God, who loved me and gave himself for me." Did you notice the "in me" and "for me" in this verse? Walking in step with the Spirit is an intensely personal journey.

Once we've shed any baggage that grieves God the Spirit, He enables us to live from God's smile, not trying to win God's smile. The Holy Spirit helps us to live from our identity as sons and daughters of the Most High God, not fight for our identity amid feelings of doubt, worthlessness, or hopelessness. The Spirit truly helps us in every way as we are swept into His embrace.

And while life in God's Spirit is very personal and intimate, the Holy Spirit also fills you not just for you but for the building up of His church. Our generous God gives us gifts of His Spirit to be used within the church. As 1 Corinthians 12:7 affirms, "To each is given the manifestation of the Spirit for the common good." There is a work in the body of Christ that no one but you can do. It's God's intention that you be filled so you can give. His power is meant to be poured out and shared. Once you discover and begin using the gifts God's Spirit has given you, you won't want to turn back. A life overflowing with God's power is so fulfilling.

If you have not yet identified what gifts the Spirit of God has placed in you, I've provided a few helpful resources in the endnotes.[2] Just remember that discovering your gifts is only one part of the equation. You were once spilled empty, but now, by the Spirit, you can live filled with plenty—plenty of the experienced love and mercy of Jesus that keep you going day-to-day and plenty of power to be used for God's kingdom purposes. Serve God with your spiritual gifts, and you'll find more purpose and fulfillment than you can possibly imagine.

Okay, deep breath. We've covered a lot of ground in this chapter, and I'm proud of you for looking at these essential truths. Let's live them out now, my friend.

TRAVELING TOGETHER

Spend some time talking with God or discussing the following with an accountability partner or small group.

- ▸ Read John 14:15–17. How does it impact you to know that God the Holy Spirit is your Helper and will be with you forever?
- ▸ Read Romans 8:26–27. The Holy Spirit prays in and through us when we don't have the words. Have you

ever experienced this? If so, what was that like? If not, why not stop and ask God to intercede through you in an area of prayer where you might feel stuck?

▸ Based on what you read, what does it mean to "quench" or "grieve" the Holy Spirit? Do you think your present thoughts or actions delight or grieve God's Spirit? What might He be calling you to change so you can move away from a spilled-empty life and toward a filled-with-plenty faith?

▸ Do you know what your spiritual gifts are? If so, are you currently using them for God's kingdom work? If not, which resources will you pursue to help on your no-turning-back journey with Jesus?

POINTS TO PONDER AS YOU PROGRESS

To be blessed is to be still.
The more time you spend slowing down and intentionally fellowshipping with the Holy Spirit, the more filled with Him you'll be. When you're filled with the Holy Spirit, you'll never thirst for the world again.

From Self-Reliance
to Relying on God's Power

> For the foolishness of God is wiser than men, and the
> weakness of God is stronger than men.
>
> 1 CORINTHIANS 1:25

A FIERCE, EARLY-SEASON ICE STORM raged through
Oklahoma, leaving thousands without power. Denisse and
I invited some dear friends whose electricity had been out
for quite some time to stay at our home, where lights, appliances, and digital devices could still draw charge. Our home
was cozy, heated, a welcome refuge from the vicious weather
and its effects. Everything was perfect—until it wasn't.

I opened my eyes and quickly realized something was
wrong . . . very wrong. I could barely move, and the pain in
my back shot across every ligament and muscle. In agonizing

slow motion, I rolled to my side and began lowering myself off the mattress. The only thing I could think was to get onto the hard surface of the floor, where my back might feel some relief. Knowing I had to find the safest place to do that, I crawled like an infant to my closet, laying myself out like a corpse on the floor beneath my wife's dresses and my own button-downs. I was incapacitated. Powerless.

I first injured my back during my Army days. My platoon had been moving ammo crates during a weekend battle assembly when pain inexplicably ricocheted across my back, leaving me gasping. I tried to continue, but it became absolutely clear that my back wouldn't bend to my will. After talking with my commander, I received leave to go home and recover. Though he told me to get treatment at the hospital, I pridefully determined what would be best was lying in bed with ice packs, popping Advil like candy and binge-watching Netflix. Since I was young and fit, my back started to regain strength relatively quickly over the next few days. I returned to active duty, but the injury simply refused to go away.

The next time I tweaked my back things got worse; the new reality of a bulging disc meant my recovery time was much longer and more painful. But, again, I did regain strength and started to return to my normal activities, including vigorous exercise. One night, while doing a Manny Pacquiao boxing workout, my disc progressed from bulging to herniated. I went from swinging and punching to drowning in agonizing pain. I had never felt the likes of it. Radiating heat, numbness, tingling, and muscle spasms took turns ravaging my body. I dropped to the floor and shouted for Denisse to help me. The pain was so intense I honestly wondered how I could keep living. My wife rushed me to the ER, but the drive and transfer felt like an eternity. The doctors and nurses offered me the help they could and sent me home. Slower than ever before, I regained strength.

Fast-forward to several weeks later, when the ice storm hit Oklahoma and I lay on the closet floor, gripped once again in the anguish of this back injury. I could do nothing—literally nothing—without help. Denisse brought me break-fast in the closet, feeding me because my arms couldn't manage to lift fork to mouth. Our friends who had come to find refuge from the weather quickly shifted from guests to helpers, serving me with such mercy in my powerless state. I couldn't even dress myself, let alone get to the car on my own so I could be seen at the emergency room. Once we got there, the ER staff placed blankets on the floor of the waiting room so I could lie down as I waited to be seen by doctors. I was completely and utterly helpless, unable even to stand up or sit down on my own.

There was nothing I could do. I had no power over this pain. I couldn't offer anyone anything. It was humbling in a way I'd never previously experienced. I'd always been "the strong one," first as a highly disciplined and powerful athlete, then as an Army officer. I wasn't used to being weak and needy. And yet, through this back injury that just wouldn't go away, I learned that there is true beauty at the end of myself.

Before my injury, I knew cognitively that Christ wanted me to depend fully on His power, not my own. I knew He wanted all of us—including me—to live with an awareness of just how much we need Him, that apart from Him we can do nothing (see John 15:5). I guess I always assumed that this truth was simply a spiritual principle, not one that needed to be worked out, to be *lived out*, in daily life.

However, coming to the utter end of my physical power, watching how beautifully my wife and my friends served me, and remembering God's Word in Matthew 23:11, "The greatest among you shall be your servant," helped me see that when I am at the end of myself, God's power is on perfect display.

WHERE WE'VE COME FROM

No one likes being powerless. The message of this chapter, "start at the end of yourself," is a tough sell for Westerners, particularly those shaped by the American dream of independence. Born and raised in the United States, I was molded by the American dream in ways I didn't even realize until I began surrendering my life to Christ. On a deep, if subconscious, level I had absorbed the idea that with enough imagination, innovation, and ingenuity I could do whatever I set my mind to doing. As I emerged into adulthood, my plans focused on getting the right degree, cultivating the perfect skill set, and climbing the ladder (or, better yet, developing the successful business) until I was at the top, in control of my own destiny. I saw no problem with this pursuit of power, and I'm definitely not alone in that life trajectory.

Even at the earliest age, we see children exerting their power in whatever ways they can. God gave Denisse and me three precious little boys who display this daily. Aiden, our eldest, makes sure his little brother, Eli, knows exactly which toys are his. If Eli dares to touch one, Aiden is quite likely to exercise power by pushing his brother to the floor. No doubt their baby brother will enter this fray all too soon.

I wonder if our desires and plays for power look as childish to God?

Children learn to wield power and control through emotional outbursts too. We call them tantrums, and woe to the parent unprepared for the tornado of a tantrum in some public space. This recently happened to Denisse and me in a Barnes & Noble bookstore, where our family often enjoys going (though Aiden and Eli less because of the books and more because of the fantastic children's area set up at the back of the store). When the time came to head home, Aiden erupted into screams that echoed through the entire building. He wanted *that fire truck*, and, let me tell you something, my son was on fire that evening. Nothing Denisse or I did would extinguish his emotional inferno. He flatly refused to leave. He wanted to use his toddler power to control what we did and to get what he wanted, when he wanted it, NOW.

Some of us never grow out of that way of exerting power, though our "tantrums" may erupt in sarcasm, manipulation, or verbal assaults. Shaped from our earliest experiences by the thought that we can get what we want, when and how we want it, if we only have enough power, we use the influence we have to put ourselves in control and on the throne.

Here's the problem: this is the exact opposite of what Christ calls His followers to do. In fact, the American dream is, in many ways, the antithesis of the gospel message. The

American dream can be described as an invitation to come and succeed; the gospel invitation, however, is a call to die, to come to the very end of ourselves. Jesus declares, "If anyone would come after me, let him deny himself and take up his cross daily and follow me" (Luke 9:23).

In the ancient world, the only thing that happened on a cross was death. There was no other option. That's why Jesus's command to take up our cross is a terminal one. But the gospel is also a call to life, to real and everlasting life. Death is simply the passageway through which Christ's followers come to share in His infinite glory and power. John 11:25 reminds us of this precious truth: "Jesus said to her, 'I am the resurrection and the life. Whoever believes in me, though he die, yet shall he live.'"

Many of us in the Western church, and I include myself in this, have been trying desperately to cling to the world and its power structures while also trying to follow Jesus. This is impossible. In order to genuinely follow in Christ's footsteps, from death through to everlasting life, we must lay down our desire for control, for power, for anything apart from God Himself.

I relied for many years on my physical strength and relational charm to control my life. I exerted power with my prowess and my smile. Coming to the end of myself physically, especially through my back injury, has been one of the best—if hardest—things that could ever happen to me.

What about you? Where has your power come from? Have you relied on your intellect, your ability to persuade, or your skill at teaching others? Have you used creativity to influence others, maybe through perfectly curated social media feeds or savvy marketing? Have you figured out how to emotionally arrange relationships in a way that allows you to get what you want from the people around you? Do you use the resources God's given you—money, time, or skill—to exert control over your life? Perhaps you've even exerted spiritual control over people, wowing them with your insights into the Scripture and your super-visible, praised-by-others gifts.

All of these things may work for a season. They may, in fact, work for many years. But relying on your own power will eventually fail you. The money dries up, followers stop watching your videos, you get old and less able to remember the deep thoughts you once taught others, people see that you've emotionally manipulated them and say, "Enough is enough." The power structures of self are doomed to destruction.

Where we've been is trying to stay at the peak of our performance, exerting our power. But where we're headed, in God's grace and mercy, is to the end of ourselves, where life itself—and God's almighty power—is found.

WHERE WE'RE HEADED

Not long after Jesus told His followers that finding real life required that they take up the cross and follow Him, an argument broke out among His closest disciples.

> And they came to Capernaum. And when [Jesus] was in the house he asked them, "What were you discussing on the

way?" But they kept silent, for on the way they had argued with one another about who was the greatest. . . . And he said to them, "If anyone would be first, he must be last of all and servant of all." (Mark 9:33–35)

I find it absolutely fascinating that Jesus doesn't scold His disciples for their impertinence, especially considering He had—only a few verses before this—predicted His own torture and death (vv. 30–32). Our gracious God doesn't shame His followers for wanting to be great but rather reveals the true path of greatness to them. As only Christ can do, He takes the disciples on a journey of discovery rather than a journey of condemnation. What a kind and wise and good God we serve!

Knowing that we've all come from a broken, sinful place where we want our way above everyone else's, Jesus tells us where to head if we want true greatness. Our Lord knows we all want to experience greatness, to have a taste of glory. But the great reversal of gospel truth is that greatness comes through service, not through wielding power.

In Jesus, we are called to willingly lay down our power. We're invited to joyfully relinquish the illusion of control. We're called to greatness by being the "servant of all."

Realistically, people don't get excited about this idea. Most of us are taught that *real life* is being served, not serving others. My coaches used to say that certain guys "had the bag." By this they meant that a guy had everything he could possibly want. NFL potential! Man, I wanted to have the bag. Especially because—at that time—my friend DJ did.

DJ, a local rapper who had become successful with a number of hot tracks, lived in one of the nicest high-rises in Kansas City. He drove the latest model luxury Mercedes. A beautiful girl was always draped on his arm as he walked through the VIP door at clubs. He dressed the wealth, drove the wealth, lived the wealth. And I wanted all that and the proverbial bag of chips. Everywhere DJ went, people served him. At hotels, he got the best room; at bars, he scored free drinks. Because he was a local kid who made it big, neighborhood people, recognizing DJ's car, would come out to honor him. I wanted that too. I wanted to be served.

So I headed in that direction. I became a hype man for a successful rapper and music producer. I started living what I thought was "the life." And it all totally fell apart. Being served wasn't what it was cracked up to be; I had to constantly "maintain" my status, my platform, my power. Nobody told me that being "on top" would be so exhausting.

When I came to Christ and discovered He wanted me to head in an entirely new direction, I was, I'll admit, a bit skeptical. *Greatness comes through serving, Lord? Really? It sure doesn't look like that in the world around me.* As I drew closer and closer to God, however, not only the trajectory of my life changed but my vision did as well. I began to see the authentic beauty of those who served willingly and completely. I watched them grow in esteem and strength. It was humbling and exciting.

The day that I lay on the floor of my closet, completely powerless and at the end of myself, I saw more clearly than ever before that the servant really is the greatest. My wife and my friends, serving me in God's strength, were far greater than I. And I rejoiced in the truth rather than fighting against it. I embraced that where I'm headed—and where you can head too—is reliance on God rather than on self. I've determined not to turn back to self-reliance or the pursuit of worldly power. What about you? I pray you'll join me in turning to God's power rather than back to the empty promises of control and independence. If you're ready to move forward, let's look at what we need to get rid of to make our journey with Jesus lighter and freer.

TRAVELING LIGHTLY

I recently received a heartbreaking email from a parent asking for prayer for an adult child who "wore pride like a necklace" and engaged in selfish, destructive behaviors, indulging in mockery and rage. Though the details are different for everyone, I believe the theme of this email—how damaging pride can be—applies to every single one of us. Whether overtly or in an upside-down way through insecurity and self-effacing comments, most of us have worn pride as a necklace at some point in life. We've all focused on ourselves more than on God and others, which is the root of a prideful heart, however it may manifest in actions and words.

C. S. Lewis describes pride as the "Great Sin." In *Mere Christianity*, he explains, "It is Pride which has been the chief cause of misery in every nation and every family since the world began." How can he make such a claim? Because "pride always means enmity (i.e., ill will, hostility). . . . And not only enmity between man and man, but enmity to God. As long as you are proud you cannot know God."[1]

If we are to know God and walk in His ways, we must shed pride. Pride weighs us down and slows our pilgrimage to the everlasting kingdom. It causes us to view those around us as competitors for limited resources, not companions on the journey with Jesus. Again, Lewis nails it with these words:

> Pride gets no pleasure out of having something, only out of having more of it than the next man. . . . It is the comparison that makes you proud: the pleasure of being above the rest. Once the element of competition is gone, pride is gone.[2]

Pride tells us we must keep others down so that we can have more and have better. Seeing that written, you may shrink back, like I'm tempted to do. *That's not who I am*, my flesh cries out. Yet, sadly, it is. Apart from Christ, I want me *above* others. In language antithetical to Jesus's words, I want to be served, not to serve.

But that is not the kingdom way. The way of Jesus is the way of glory, true. However, this way involves death that leads to life and service that leads to greatness. It's the greatest of reversals, the gospel truth.

If we're to travel lightly with Christ and to our everlasting home in God's presence, we must willingly and deliberately cast off pride and the self-reliance that comes with it. Pride, being the opposite of humility, must rely on self to accomplish its purposes. According to Jesus, however, pride is a liar and always will be. Christ told His disciples and tells us twenty-first-century, independent-minded people: "I am the vine; you are the branches. Whoever abides in me and I in him, he it is that bears much fruit, for apart from me you can do nothing" (John 15:5).

Pride cannot maintain dominion over you when you know that, apart from Jesus, you can do nothing. That's why the dear sister who emailed me about her prideful son understands correctly that "only God and genuine prayer can help."

If I were to guess, I'd say that fear is the biggest reason people hold on to self-reliance and pride. We're so desperately afraid of being out of control, afraid of losing what power we think we've worked so hard to have. Instead of fearing the loss of control, we're invited by God to "perfect love [that] casts out fear" (1 John 4:18). Instead of clinging to pride and self, we're called by God to remember that lasting victory comes "not by might, nor by power, but by my Spirit, says the LORD of hosts" (Zech. 4:6).

I recognize it's difficult to imagine willingly laying down your power, your control, your influence. When you do, however, you'll see it was all an illusion anyway, carefully and diabolically maintained to keep you in bondage to self. Jesus is our perfect example of traveling lightly, free of pride and self-reliance.

Read with me the words of Philippians 2:5–9.

Have this mind among yourselves, which is yours in Christ Jesus, who, though he was in the form of God, did not count equality with God a thing to be grasped, but emptied himself, by taking the form of a servant, being born in the likeness of men. And being found in human form, he humbled himself by becoming obedient to the point of death, even death on a cross. Therefore God has highly exalted him and bestowed on him the name that is above every name.

Jesus willingly and humbly emptied Himself, letting go of what He deserved—all glory, honor, and power. He did not grasp or posture. He became the chief servant, obedient to death. And *then* God highly exalted Him.

If you would be great, like your Lord, let go of pride and walk free of self-reliance. This is the key to traveling lightly along the way. To travel wisely as you go, let's look at how you can practically rely on God's power rather than your own.

TRAVELING WISELY

As we let go of pride and self-reliance, we must simultaneously and deliberately embrace God's power. And we do this best through personal, intimate, and ongoing prayer. To help you remember four practical and essential ways to rely on God's strength rather than on your own, I've created an acronym bringing these two together: P.R.A.Y. When you pray, you align yourself with God's strength rather than your own. You shift allegiance from self to God. And, in coming to the end of yourself, you will find more than you could have asked for or even imagined (see Eph. 3:20).

To travel wisely on the road to glory in Jesus, remember to P.R.A.Y.

P Is for Presence

The presence of God will always be greater than your greatest performance, possessions, platforms, or prize. The treasure of God's nearness is vastly superior to the gifts of this world, and His riches last for all eternity. His closeness goes beyond death. The psalmist Asaph writes,

> Whom have I in heaven but you?
>> And there is nothing on earth that I desire
>> besides you.
> My flesh and my heart may fail,
>> but God is the strength of my heart and my
>> portion forever. . . .
> But for me it is good to be near God;
>> I have made the Lord God my refuge,
>> that I may tell of all your works. (73:25–26, 28)

I have learned that "for me it is good to be near God." Have you learned this yet? If not, it's time. God's nearness keeps you from turning back to the empty promises of the world.

R Is for Rest

Do you feel weary from trying so hard to control everything, striving to hold life together? Are you falling apart, burdened by expectations or failures? You can take Jesus up on His offer of rest (see Matt. 11:28). It never expires and there's no payment required. There's only one prerequisite to God's rest: "Come." Come to His open and gentle heart today. Rest from the pressure of power seeking and self-aggrandizing. It's no wonder people are constantly exhausted, anxious, and depressed; relying on our own strength will always lead to this kind of pain and frustration. God's rest, on the other hand, is a gift of grace. It's never a transaction. Because your joyful rest starts and ends in God's presence, not your power, you can come to the end of yourself, find rest, and be empowered all at the same time. How amazing is that?

A Is for Attention

Pause. Not just for the sake of stopping, though in our increasingly frantic culture, stopping is good in and of itself. I'm asking you to pause for something even deeper. If you want to embrace God's power, pause and prepare yourself to pay attention to God. Give Him your full, undivided attention. Whatever lures your mind's attention and your heart's affections away from God will prove disastrous. With deceptive attraction, self-reliance will drain you empty and cut you into pieces. Hebrews 12:2 invites us to *fix our eyes* on Jesus, the author and finisher of our faith. If we want to experience God's far greater power at work in and through us, we must fix our attention on God. For me, it is a terrifying thought that I could use the precious gifts of time and attention to commit adultery against the Most High God. Instead, I want to be faithful to Him, the lover of my soul, by keeping my attention on Him. What about you?

Y Is for Yearn

We must yearn to see and savor God's strength more than our own. Do you spend more time thinking about Him or yourself? Do you dwell more on what you can or want to get done or what He might want to do in and through you? I've found greater joy in admiring His strength rather than exaggerating my own power. Life has the deepest meaning and joy and is sweetest when our hearts freely exalt God's power rather than boasting in our own. Do you yearn to know God's power perfected in your weakness, as 2 Corinthians 12:9–10 reveals? That's a challenging question for many of us. But our weakness humbly drives us to experience this precious truth:

> For what we proclaim is not ourselves, but Jesus Christ as Lord, with ourselves as your servants for Jesus' sake. . . . We have this treasure in jars of clay, to show that the surpassing power belongs to God and not to us. (2 Cor. 4:5, 7)

Let's be a people who do not yearn to see how great we can be but rather yearn to magnify the greatness of God. With the psalmist, let us

> Ascribe to the LORD, O families of the peoples,
>   ascribe to the LORD glory and strength!
> Ascribe to the LORD the glory due his name;
>   bring an offering, and come into his courts!
> Worship the LORD in the splendor of holiness;
>   tremble before him, all the earth! (96:7–9)

If you yearn for anything more than the glory of God, you're selling yourself—and, even more significantly, the Lord Himself—short. Yearn for His kingdom to come and His will to be done, and you will find great joy.

As you draw near to God and relish His presence, rest in Him, pay attention to Him more than anything else, and yearn for His glory above all else, your journey will be lighter, freer, and wiser. You'll be able to let go of pride, the need to exert control, and the fear of losing power. And that, my friend, is why deciding to P.R.A.Y. is the ultimate win-win situation.

TRAVELING TOGETHER

Spend some time talking with God or discussing the following with an accountability partner or small group.

- Everyone wields power in unique ways. How have you been tempted to rely on your own strength throughout life?
- Spend some time reflecting on the "Traveling Lightly" section. In what ways is Jesus currently inviting you to lay down pride and self-reliance?
- Which of the practical steps—P.R.A.Y.—to relying on God's power, not your own, is most helpful to you? How might you start practicing it today?
- Read Psalm 20. What does this psalm teach about power? How do verses 7–8 fit with what you read in this chapter?

POINTS TO PONDER AS YOU PROGRESS

Highs and lows are a sign of life; flatlining is for the dead.

God gives us life freely and powerfully.

Jesus got weary, yet He is our rest.

Jesus wept, yet He wipes away our tears.

Jesus got hungry, yet He is the Bread of Life.

Jesus got thirsty, yet He is the Living Water.

Jesus died, yet He destroyed the power of death.

Jesus is the power source of our lives.

Our strength is limited; God's strength
is unending and perfect.

Relying on Him gives us confidence to stay on the path.

From Slavery to Kinship

Yet to all who did receive him, to those who believed in his name, he gave the right to become children of God.

JOHN 1:12 NIV

IT WAS 1989. The Berlin Wall came down, tanks rolled into Tiananmen Square as nearly one million students protested communist rule in China, South Africa's wicked apartheid system crumbled, and the first draft of a proposal for what eventually would be called the World Wide Web surfaced at a nuclear research facility in Geneva.

Meanwhile, in the small, Florida panhandle town of Quincy, Freddie Figgers was born.

Who would have ever guessed this baby boy would be found next to a dumpster, abandoned and in distress? I can understand a baby being born in a manger or a run-down medical facility. But for Freddie to be born next to a mouse-infested dumpster—for just a vulnerable baby, that is about as dim as being born in a mortuary. *Scary!*

Baby Freddie spent a couple days in the hospital, being treated for minor injuries and checked for everything else. Then Nathan and Betty Figgers, who had fostered several other children and had a daughter of their own, accepted the orphaned infant into their home. Freddie was the only foster child they adopted.

You probably know what happens while rolling through a small town. Exactly nothing at all. This is what the Figgers family was used to. Have you ever heard of Quincy? Probably not—until now.

The news of Freddie's origins was no secret in such a small town. Years passed and the community still buzzed with the news of Freddie's birth and abandonment; people never stopped talking about "that poor baby." Even after Freddie grew old enough to hear and understand his story, Quincy residents kept the gossip going. Eventually, other children began bullying young Freddie at school, nicknaming him "dumpster baby."

Freddie's father, Nathan, decided the boy needed a hobby to keep him out of trouble, so he encouraged him to tinker around with a broken computer he brought home. Freddie became proficient, and by the time he was a teenager, he had a part-time job fixing computers. Soon he had more than a hundred clients.

Now he has his own company.

In an interview with the *Washington Post*, Freddie Figgers acknowledged, "My parents adopted me and gave me love and a future. . . . They did their best to make the world a better place, and now that's all I want to do, too."[1] Figgers created a unique tracking device to help families with loved ones who, suffering from Alzheimer's, might become lost and confused. It sold for $2.2 million. In 2019, a similar project of Freddie's, aimed at helping families with homeless relatives, was in development.[2]

As an adult, Freddie Figgers discovered his birth mother was a prostitute who battled drug addiction. He knew all too well, "That could be me on the streets—I could have been homeless or dead if I hadn't been found by the dumpster after I was born."[3] He was born the son of a woman enslaved to drugs and a pimp who used her. He became, through adoption, the beloved son of a father who wanted the best for Freddie, provided for him, and set him on a path of abundant life.

Unfortunately, most abandoned babies don't end up millionaires like Freddie Figgers. Many die of exposure or abuse. It takes a lot to crawl out of a bad beginning. For those deserted children who do survive, mental health struggles related to their desertion, addictions, and broken relationships often haunt their lives.

The spiritual implications for us are strikingly similar. But for the grace of God, every single one of us could have been abandoned in the garbage of sin. And without our heavenly Father, who adopted us into His family and made us heirs with His Son of the glorious riches of heaven, our stories would have ended with grief and pain.

But God.

Those awesome two words turn the tide of so much of our pain.

Our stories could have been about abandonment or enslavement to any number of sins, *but God* rescued us and set us on the path of everlasting life. As God's beloved children, we don't have to be marked by the garbage of our past lives. For many of us, however, it's a long and sometimes difficult journey away from slavery and into kinship.

If you've ever struggled to know God as your loving Father or be known by Him, this chapter is for you. When you know you're a child of God, giving in to old temptations ceases to be an option. A no-turning-back life is a move away from slavery and into kinship.

WHERE WE'VE COME FROM

In the book of Ezekiel, God gives a striking word picture describing what it's like to be born into sin:

> On the day you were born, no one cared about you. Your umbilical cord was not cut, and you were never washed, rubbed with salt, and wrapped in cloth. No one had the slightest interest in you; no one pitied you or cared for you. On the day you were born, you were unwanted, dumped in a field and left to die.
>
> But I came by and saw you there, helplessly kicking about in your own blood. As you lay there, I said, "Live!" And I helped you to thrive like a plant in the field. You grew up and became a beautiful jewel. (16:4–7 NLT)

In other words, being born in sin is a whole lot like being born in a dumpster. I'm eternally thankful that our loving

God refused to leave us there. Instead, He speaks life to us and enables us to thrive.

The first move away from the slavery of sin to kinship with Christ comes when God calls us. It may sound simplistic, but you cannot become a child of God without responding to His call. God is the perfect gentleman and will not force His love and care on anyone. He speaks life to everyone enslaved to sin, but not all receive His invitation. This is why not everyone is a child of God. Every single human is a beloved creation of the King of Kings, imprinted with His priceless, glorious image. Children of God, however, have accepted His gift of life everlasting.

Before I became a son of God, I was addicted and enslaved to porn, people pleasing, alcohol, marijuana, pride, depression, you name it. I wasn't enslaved to all of these at once. The enemy would run me through different cycles of slavery—maybe so I'd think I had victory and wouldn't run to God. Whatever the evil one's diabolical purposes, God's purposes were greater still.

Where have you been? In what dumpster have you been found? Have you truly cried out to God for rescue? If not, this is your moment. You can bow your head right now and pray, "Jesus, I need You. I see the emptiness of my life. I have been in the garbage of sin too long. I receive the gift of life You offer through Your death and resurrection for me. Please save me and teach me how to live like You."

According to Romans 8, anyone and everyone who calls on the name of the Lord in this way becomes a child of God. Hallelujah!

For all who are led by the Spirit of God are sons of God. For you did not receive the spirit of slavery to fall back into fear, but you have received the Spirit of adoption as sons, by whom we cry, "Abba! Father!" The Spirit himself bears witness with our spirit that we are children of God, and if children, then heirs—heirs of God and fellow heirs with Christ, provided we suffer with him in order that we may also be glorified with him. (vv. 14–17)[4]

By the Holy Spirit's grace and power, we get to approach the Almighty God as our Abba. This word, *Abba*, is a personal, intimate term, similar to our English words *Papa* or *Daddy*. It connotes a closeness and childlike dependence on a trusted Father. Rather than approaching God the Father in fear, which Romans 8 identifies as the spirit of slavery, we are invited as children to come near to our Abba, to receive from Him the inheritance of eternity.

Wow. What unfathomably good news!

Because we have this intimacy with our heavenly Father, we don't have to be intimidated when we face the world every day. Kinship means security. Kinship means confidence.

In the morning, when you rise up, do you feel like a son or daughter of your loving Abba? Are you confident and secure in your Father's love? If so, I rejoice with you! If not, why not?

I believe one of the key dynamics of our journey away from slavery and to kinship is identifying orphan thinking. You may have grown up in a perfectly respectable, perhaps even loving, home and still feel like an orphan, abandoned and unloved by your heavenly Father. Maybe a tragedy struck your life and you simply can't shake the grief or resentment. Maybe things looked good on the outside of your home, but the inner turmoil, the slavery to a cycle of abuse, addiction, anxiety, or anger festered in your heart.

Many of us have been stuck in an orphan mindset. Orphans have to rely on their own wits to get through life. They beg, barter, steal . . . whatever they can to get ahead. They have to look out for themselves because no one else will. Nothing will be given to them, so they work tirelessly to earn. Spiritual orphans are enslaved, perhaps not to substances but to self-reliance.

You can recognize orphan thinking by a fixation on *want*. Nothing is ever enough. Negativity is prevalent. Many with an orphan mindset become obsessed with being affirmed by others and being liked and admired. In an already competitive culture, those mired in orphan thinking restlessly claw their way to success. Spiritual orphans are often enslaved to their desires for more and better, though nothing seems to prove their worth or satisfy them.

The Bible teaches us that children of God say no to orphan thinking and abide in the Father's loving arms. Don't get caught up in that biblical word as if it's difficult to understand. *Abide* simply means to make yourself at home in, to trust in, to lean on. A son or daughter of God feels at home in the Abba's embrace, trusts in the heavenly Father's purposes, and leans on Him for guidance and grace.

I recently watched a difficult-to-view but very powerful miniseries about African slavery titled *Roots*. Based on the bestselling book of the same name by Alex Haley, this series follows the story of a Gambian teenager, Kunta Kinte, who is kidnapped and sold into bondage in Colonial America. Bought by a plantation owner, he works the vast grounds with other slaves owned by "the master." They are separated from family life, off in the corners of the fields, working day and night to utter exhaustion.

Something clicked for me while watching Kunta Kinte's struggles toward freedom. He and all the other slaves were kept away from the master's house. They knew none of the master's plans. They received none of his affection. All of that was reserved for the master's children. Though this rarely, if ever, happened in the actual world of African slavery, at any moment the master could have rescued the slaves and made them joint heirs of his fortune through adoption.

That didn't happen to Kunta Kinte, but that is a lot like what happened to me. Why on earth would I continue living like a slave, trying to earn scraps of favor from a feared master who might beat me if I stepped out of line? Why would I live and work away from the true Master, separated from His presence, His affection, and His plans that are good for me? Do you see where I'm heading?

I don't think we intend to live as spiritual orphans. I do think, however, that's where many of us have been, and—sadly—I think it's where many believers still live. They have received Christ as Lord and have been adopted by God, but they are still living with an orphan mindset. They're out with the slaves, not in the house with the children.

It's time for all God's kids to come in and come close. It's time to say no—for good—to the orphan mindset and start looking forward to what's in store.

WHERE WE'RE HEADED

If where we've been is the dumpster of sin and mired in an orphan mindset, where are we headed? What does it truly mean to live as a beloved child of God? What does it mean to have a kinship mindset?

In an encounter with the ultrareligious yet completely hypocritical Pharisees, Jesus contrasted the place of a child and the place of a slave. The Pharisees bristled at being told they were in bondage to their sin, but Jesus replied, "Very truly I tell you, everyone who sins is a slave to sin. Now a slave has no permanent place in the family, but a son belongs to it forever. So if the Son sets you free, you will be free indeed" (John 8:34–36 NIV).

Being a child of God involves belonging, freedom, and permanence.

Belonging gives the sons and daughters of God confidence and peace. They don't have to strive to prove themselves or please everyone around them. As I've said before, they don't live *for* God's smile but *from* it. They know their Abba delights in them, just as Psalm 147:11 declares: "The LORD delights in those who fear him, who put their hope in his unfailing love" (NIV).

I experienced the incredible power of knowing I belonged during my first year as an officer in the US Army. As a newly minted second lieutenant, I earned favor with my commanding officer and was given the tremendous honor of shadowing a visiting general—one of the top-ranking officials in the entire nation—during his visit to our base.

My uniform had never been crisper, my shoes shinier, or my palms sweatier. The temperature hovered somewhere around a zillion degrees Fahrenheit that summer day in Fort Knox, Kentucky, and my whole body tensed with heat and adrenaline. I was scared out of my mind that I'd do something wrong, something humiliating.

Things actually went quite well until the general and I headed to what I had been informed would be a very important meeting. I had also been told I would be the youngest and lowest-ranking officer in the room. Let me tell you; I felt the pressure. And then I realized I'd forgotten my notebook and pen back at the command center.

There was nothing for it. I had to address the general.

"Sir," I said, standing at attention.

"Yes, Lieutenant."

"Permission to retrieve my pen and notebook from the command center, sir."

I waited for the hammer to fall.

"Roger that. Make it pronto."

Hugely relieved, I looked at my watch. I had two minutes until the meeting began. I raced back, grabbed what I needed, about-faced, and sprinted again. Once I reached the building where the meeting would take place, I slowed to the fastest speed-walk humanly possible, not wanting to draw too much attention to myself by running in the corridors. I *so* did not want to be "that guy," the newbie who embarrassed the base.

As I approached the meeting room, I realized I was one minute late. My heart sank until I noticed that the door was still open. They had waited for me. I could hardly contain my relief at that moment.

Just as I was about to cross the threshold into the room, a lieutenant colonel barked at me, "Lieutenant, what are you doing here?"

"Sir. I was invited, sir."

"No. You don't belong here," he growled. "You need to go."

Before I could reply, the lieutenant colonel was pushed aside by none other than the general.

"He's with me. Come in, Lieutenant Copeland."

Despite what the lieutenant colonel believed, I *did* belong there. I had been invited. I was received. I was vouched for and secure. I had access because of the general. And even though I had made a mistake, a mistake that made me late for this important meeting, I wasn't condemned or cast out. The door was open; I was defended when accused. I *belonged*.

Joyfully walking beside the general to my seat at the table, I realized how powerful it is to know that you belong. I didn't attend every important meeting at Fort Knox from then on; I belonged that day because of the general, but my place at the table wasn't a forever thing.

How much more powerful is it to know that we belong— eternally, without the possibility of being rejected—to and with the King of Kings, the God of Angel Armies, the Everlasting One? Because of Jesus, we get access to places and privileges that we could never deserve. Because we are loved and valued by our heavenly Father, we belong *forever*.

According to John 8:36, this eternal security brings great freedom. "If the Son sets you free, you will be free indeed." You are no longer a slave; you are a child of God. As the apostle John wrote later in his life, "See what great love the

Father has lavished on us, that we should be called children of God! And that is what we are!" (1 John 3:1 NIV). Children of God, lavished with love . . . that is who we are! If that doesn't amaze you, check your pulse.

On our journey with Jesus, bumps and bruises may abound, but our belonging never changes. We are accepted forever, without exception. This secures freedom for us. In order to really live in that freedom, however, we need to cast off any garbage that, coming out of the dumpster of sin, has been left clinging to us. Let's take the trash out now.

TRAVELING LIGHTLY

Though many things can keep us locked in an orphan mindset, I'd like to focus on one major one in this section: the misrepresentation of God our heavenly Father through our imperfect earthly parents. Some who read this book will have grown up in lovely homes with great families. Others carry the pain of years of hurt, disappointment, anger, and/ or abuse. Whichever group you fall into, the reality is no parent is perfect.

There are ways in which your view of God is impacted by who your earthly parents are. And without taking the initiative to forgive our earthly parents, there is no progress. Too many Christians are walking around as spiritual orphans because, in their hurt and confusion, they've divorced themselves from their earthly parents and suffered in their relationship with their Abba.

When we fail to forgive others, we don't experience the love of the Father because resentment sets up obstacles between us. Bitterness and unforgiveness don't only separate us from one another, though they certainly do that in horrible ways. They also suffocate our intimacy with God; our minds and thoughts are far from our heavenly Father when we're stuck in the pain of our pasts.

To move past our pasts on our journey with Jesus, forgiveness is the only option. Perhaps, you protest, you don't really know where to begin. That's completely relatable. I've been there.

Forgiving others always begins with receiving forgiveness ourselves. Without the forgiveness of Jesus settled in our hearts, there is no way to genuinely forgive another human. That's why God uses His gift of forgiveness to guide us: "Be kind to one another, tenderhearted, forgiving one another, as God in Christ forgave you" (Eph. 4:32). Notice the Lord doesn't say, "Forgive because I told you to." He invites us to forgive because He's done it for us. Forgiveness isn't something we have to white-knuckle or conjure up. Forgiveness is a flow that comes from Jesus to us, then out of us to others.

Just because forgiveness comes from the Father and flows out from Him doesn't make it easy. It can be incredibly painful. Don't forget; the forgiveness of my sin and yours cost Jesus His life. His death was brutal and cruel. Forgiveness is the free gift of God, but it's not cheap. Thankfully, we never walk the path of forgiveness on our own. God the Father went before us in sending His Son; Jesus showed us the way through His death and resurrection; and the Spirit guides us as we walk, even when we walk wounded.

If you want to forgive, it may surprise you to learn that one way to move forward is to experience forgiveness yourself. If there is someone you've hurt, asking for and receiving their forgiveness can help your own resentful heart begin to thaw.

Though this story may not be typical, here's how it happened for me.

My nana—my father's wonderful mother—lay dying from cancer in a hospital hundreds of miles away. I adored my father's steadying, guiding presence in my youth; it was exactly what I needed. But when I got older and he got older, I judged him—*He wasn't there for us; he sometimes had a beer too many*, I thought—with the harsh eye of a teenage know-it-all. You know the type.

But now . . . he needed me. I drove as fast as the law allowed so that I could be with my dad and say goodbye to his mom, my amazing nana.

As Dad and I sat on Nana's porch after she passed, something welled up inside me.

"Dad, I need you to forgive me."

My father looked me square in the face. Not one muscle twitched.

"What do you mean? Forgive you for what?"

"I put you and Mom through so much. You bailed me out of jail. You stood in the hospital, scared out of your mind that I would die because of my own stupidity. I did pretty much everything you told me not to do."

My father didn't say anything.

"I said I'd help Nana make the car payments, Dad, but I ran off to LA and drove her credit score down. I'm hurting for it now. I'm so sorry, Dad. Please forgive me."

The tears started to roll down his face.

"No. I won't forgive you."

What? The old resentment clawed at the doors of my heart. *This man who chose alcohol over our family again and again . . . he won't forgive me? The guy who hurt me and missed way more of my games than he ever came to . . . he's not going to forgive me?* I knew Jesus had forgiven me. I knew He was calling me to forgive my dad. This hurt, though.

"I won't forgive you, son. Until you forgive me."

Shock momentarily paralyzed me. Then joy flooded my whole being and I hugged my dad, knowing that I had finally forgiven him. His own father had told him he wanted nothing to do with him. That must have been so painful. My dad walked most of his life with that father wound. Through forgiveness, he and I could break that cycle.

To travel lightly on your journey with Jesus, you've got to cast off any bitterness and resentment that are keeping you from experiencing the lavish love your heavenly Father has for you. You may not experience what I did with one of your earthly parents. Your mom and dad may already have passed. Circumstances or safety concerns may mean that seeking them out for a heart-to-heart like I had with my father simply isn't possible. The good news: you can walk the road of forgiveness no matter what situation presently confronts you. Seeking forgiveness from someone other than your parents may help you on this journey. Receiving forgiveness from Christ first and then from a friend or family member whom you hurt can make forgiving those who have wounded you more possible.

Travel lightly. Discover the freedom of forgiveness, and the lavish love of your heavenly Father will be more real to you every day.

TRAVELING WISELY

As we put off unforgiveness in order to more fully embrace our identity as sons and daughters of God, we also need to put on knowledge of who our heavenly Father is. Without knowing His character, we may inadvertently revert to an orphan mindset.

Jesus told a parable about two sons who misunderstood their loving father. Whereas our earthly parents disappoint and hurt us, necessitating forgiveness, the story Jesus relates in Luke 15 is entirely different. The father in this story makes no false move, yet both his sons live with an orphan mindset.

I'm describing, of course, the parable of the prodigal son, who asks his father to give him his inheritance so that he can live as he pleases, far away from his family. The father agrees to his younger son's request, and the inheritance is quickly squandered in reckless living. Coming to his senses while starving in a pigpen, envying the slop of the swine around him, the younger son returns to his homeland thinking he will hire himself to his father, whose servants eat better than the pigs he tended in that foreign land. Instead of becoming a slave to his father, the younger son is greeted by a dad who runs toward him with arms open, heart open, wallet open. He kills the fatted calf to throw a party for his son, puts a ring and robe on him, and welcomes him back to his identity as a son. That security had been his all along, even when he willingly walked away from it.

The story is plenty powerful if we stop there, though the impact is even more intense when we compare the response of the elder son after his brother comes back. Luke 15:28–32 tells us:

> But he was angry and refused to go in [to the celebration]. His father came out and entreated him, but he answered his father, "Look, these many years I have served you, and I never disobeyed your command, yet you never gave me a young goat, that I might celebrate with my friends. But when this son of yours came, who has devoured your property with prostitutes, you killed the fattened calf for him!" And he said to him, "Son, you are always with me, and all that is mine is yours. It was fitting to celebrate and be glad, for this your brother was dead, and is alive; he was lost, and is found."

Both brothers misunderstood their father. The younger son believed he could lose his father's love, while the older son believed he could earn or deserve it. Both sons cut off intimacy with their father by not knowing him as he truly was: lavishly loving, merciful, and gracious. Both boys lived with an orphan mindset. Before his return home, the younger son saw his father only as a means to an end. He didn't care about the father's love, only getting what he wanted. The older son saw his dad as a harsh taskmaster, difficult to please and expecting constant perfection. Both suffered in these misunderstandings.

It's radical to realize that Jesus's parable only shows the father as loving and good. There is absolutely no indication given to support either brother's viewpoint. Our heavenly Father is only loving and good. And yet so many of us cut off intimacy with Him because we don't understand Him.

Our Abba has given us everything we need to get to know Him. His Spirit dwells within us and gives us the mind of Jesus (see 1 Cor. 2:16). He's given us His Word, which keeps us out of the dumpster of sin and reveals His goodness to us. "Before I was afflicted I went astray," the psalmist proclaims, "but now I keep your word. You are good and do good; teach me your statutes" (119:67–68).

If you want to travel wisely, get to know your Abba. Make yourself at home in Him. Let Him be at home in you. We'll look at this more over the next couple chapters. Let nothing infect your intimacy with the heavenly Father. Forgive freely, abandon the orphan mindset, and live as the child of God you truly are.

TRAVELING TOGETHER

Spend some time talking with God or discussing the following with an accountability partner or small group.

- ▶ Do you currently have more of an orphan mindset or a kinship mindset? Why? Explore this with God the Holy Spirit through prayer or journaling.
- ▶ Is it easy or difficult for you to believe that, as a child of God, you belong and are free . . . permanently? Why?

- ▶ Resentment breaks our intimacy with the heavenly Father. Who is God calling you to forgive? From whom is He inviting you to ask forgiveness?
- ▶ In what ways are you presently getting to know your Abba? Are there ways in which you may have misunderstood Him? In what ways could you grow in your understanding of who He is?

POINTS TO PONDER AS YOU PROGRESS

Scripture doesn't say, "Become a son or daughter of God, and you'll be free of pain and problems." However, it does say that nothing in all of the universe is outside the sovereign control of our heavenly Father. Fixing your eyes on the prize of His presence guarantees your path will always lead to the promise.

From Dying Religion to Living Relationship

> Now this is eternal life: that they know you, the only
> true God, and Jesus Christ, whom you have sent.
>
> JOHN 17:3 NIV

IMAGINE THIS.

You come to, dizzy and disoriented but keenly aware that's something's wrong. Very wrong. When you sit up, a cold, wet wave breaks over the lower half of your body. Quick glances left, right, and behind you fill in some details. You're on the shore of an island, apparently alone. This isn't the vacation you were promised.

What happened? Why are you here? What are you supposed to do now? Why are your thoughts so confused?

Your injuries seem minor and the sun is beating down on you, so you get up, determined to do something other than surrender to despair. You walk inland, toward what looks like a tropical forest. It's tough going and the threat of desperation is all too real, but you press on, dialing in all five senses to collect any helpful information.

A rustling sound from your left. A grunt from somewhere ahead and to your right. You brace yourself for . . . what? A fight? An animal?

Two other men break into a clearing as you enter it as well. For a moment, all three of you size each other up, estimating potential danger. You then throw your hands up in a gesture of peace and address yourself to the strangers.

"Do you know where we are?"

You quickly form a bond with these other stranded travelers. Your arrival stories are different, but all of you agree that getting off this island is imperative. You don't know precisely why, but it feels like a matter of life and death. Together, you journey farther inland.

Your conversation centers on suggestions for what to do and when to do it. You don't share very many personal details, not because you're suspicious—they both seem like good guys—but only because there's a much bigger fish to fry: How are you going to survive?

Thankfully, one of the guys has a backpack with him, and he has enough water for each of you to drink a few ounces, which is definitely a good thing, as you've been walking for a couple hours in the heat of the day. Just when you think you can't make it much farther, the undergrowth starts to thin. Your foot hits asphalt, broken up by years' worth of weeds. What on earth?

You start to run as the reality hits you . . . this means civilization. There's hope here. The other guys are right behind you as you break into a huge, open area. A runway stretches into the distance and a small propeller plane waits at the opposite end. It appears to be in good condition. All three of you are giddy with excitement, though something's nagging at the back at your mind. *Who's going to fly us out of here?*

"Don't worry, I can fly this plane," the guy on your right says, breathless from racing but brimming with confidence.

"I'm a pilot," the man on your left says, quieter perhaps but with no less confidence.

By the time you've gotten to the plane, you've heard all about how the guy on your right grew up in a family of pilots. Now that you've stopped, he pulls a fading photograph of an older man and young boy in front of a WWII biplane from his pocket.

"This is me and my grandfather," he says, pointing. "War hero. Flying is in my blood."

The other man is busy looking the plane over, evaluating its condition.

"Good thing I always carry this with me," the man with the photograph says as he pulls a leather-bound volume from his backpack. You glimpse the words "A Comprehensive Guide to Flight" as he opens the heavy book. "If we follow this carefully, we'll be out of here in no time," he assures you.

The other man is now in the cockpit, adjusting dials and gauges.

"Are you sure you know how to fly this plane?" you ask the first man, who is flipping through the flight manual. In response, he flashes a cocky smile, reaches down to the hem of his shirt, pulls it off, and turns around in one swift motion.

"This is all the proof you need," he states, flexing his back muscles so that the wings tattooed on his lats move up and down.

The engine roars to life. The propeller spins. The plane swings around slowly, now pointing down the runway. The quiet guy leans out the window and calls, "Come with me if you want to live."

Wait. Is this a movie scene?

"I'm the way home," he adds.

What do you do next?

WHERE WE'VE COME FROM

My island story is a parable of sorts. We're all on a journey; sometimes we don't know where we're going. Sin disorients and injures us. It leaves us stranded, like confused travelers who believe their destination should have been paradise. An impending sense of doom pushes us to seek escape. It feels like a matter of life and death because it is. Eternity is at stake.

The two men you stumbled across in this parable represent two offers of escape from the wilderness of sin. You want to get to your true home—this is the promise of the gospel—but who do you trust to guide you there? You can go with the guy who seems to have all the right credentials. He's got the "look" and the "book" and the confidence to boot. But the other guy, quiet as he is, actually gets the plane started. He's walking the talk, so to speak, not just talking it up.

The point of this little parable of mine is that, at some point in your Christian journey, you're going to have to choose between two offers: one from the law and one from grace. Both make promises of deliverance. Only one leads to life.

Put in such direct terms, it's probably pretty obvious which guy you can trust to get you home. Maybe there are nagging doubts in your mind, though. You haven't actually seen this guy fly, even though he's the one who got the plane going and can maneuver it down the runway at least. You may still feel vulnerable getting in the plane. I understand that.

In our story, the guy with "flying in his blood" represents the promise of the law. The law has the right pedigree. It's based on a manual for flight. It's got the right appearance and is cocky in its confidence. Similarly, the Pharisees of Jesus's day—the "teachers of the law" as they are often called in Scripture—religiously followed "the book," a list of over six hundred laws from the Mosaic Scriptures, their "Comprehensive Manual for Righteousness." They had the spiritual pedigrees—righteousness was in their blood—and they told people to follow them. They put on great shows of righteousness, praying long and loudly in public, like men flexing their spiritual muscles. But a show is all it ever was. Following the law is a road to nowhere; it did not and will *never* lead to life.

Sometimes it feels risky to accept the other invitation, the one to grace. There's no absolute proof that grace "flies"; it requires faith. I can tell you all about my journey off the island of sin in the hands of grace. You can hear from others too. But ultimately you have to decide whether you're getting in the plane or not.

What changes everything is realizing that Jesus is your pilot. Like the two travelers on the road to Emmaus who didn't recognize Jesus (see Luke 24:13–35), you may not realize at first that the offer of grace is from your Savior. In some ways, it seems too good to be true. *You mean I don't even have to spend one night on this island? I don't have to work for it? Can it really be as easy as trusting in faith?*

Yes, it can.

Where we've all been is marooned by sin. Where we're headed, if we'll take the offer of grace, is a living relationship of faith. We could also follow the leading of the law, but that path—while it may look good—is the path of dying religion. Let's take a closer look at where each path heads. My prayer is that, if you haven't already chosen which path to follow, examining the invitations of law and grace will make your choice that much clearer.

WHERE WE'RE HEADED

A couple thousand years ago, the apostle Paul discussed legalism and grace with his Christian brothers and sisters in Galatia. Through Paul, God revealed that those who depend on the law to make them right with God are under his curse, for the Scriptures say, "Cursed is everyone who does not observe and obey all the commands that are written in God's Book of the Law." So it is clear that no one can be made right with God by trying to keep the law. For the Scriptures say, "It is through faith that a righteous person has life." This way of faith is very different from the way of law, which says, "It is through obeying the law that a person has life."

But Christ has rescued us from the curse pronounced by the law. When he was hung on the cross, he took upon himself the curse for our wrongdoing. For it is written in the Scriptures, "Cursed is everyone who is hung on a tree." Through Christ Jesus, God has blessed the Gentiles with the same blessing he promised to Abraham, so that we who are believers might receive the promised Holy Spirit through faith. (Gal. 3:10–14 NLT)

The blessing of Abraham Paul refers to in this passage is the covenant promise that God would call and preserve for Himself a chosen people whom He would redeem from the curse of death. The Lord promised Abraham that He would bless him to be a blessing to others. This covenant was based on God's righteousness and His grace, *not* on Abraham's goodness or ability to "stick with the program." The promise of covenant grace initially extended to one man, Abraham, then his family, his tribe, and ultimately his nation. That's great for them, but what about us? Galatians 3 discloses the Good News: in Jesus, the promise of covenant grace is for all people, Jews and Gentiles alike.

Paul seems to anticipate an objection that naturally arises in a lot of people's minds. "Why, then, was the law given?" he continues in his letter to the Galatians (v. 19 NLT). Fortunately, Paul also gives us God's explanation:

It was given alongside the promise to show people their sins. But the law was designed to last only until the coming of the child who was promised. . . . Is there a conflict, then, between God's law and God's promises? Absolutely not! If the law could give us new life, we could be made right with God by obeying it. But the Scriptures declare that we are all prisoners of sin, so we receive God's promise of freedom only by believing in Jesus Christ. (vv. 19, 21–22 NLT)

In ancient times, the law fulfilled—and still fulfills today, in the twenty-first century—an incredibly important purpose: it helps us realize we have never done and can never do things perfectly. The main purpose of the law is to point us back, again and again, to our desperate need for God.

In part, that's why Jesus reserved His harshest words for the teachers of the law who put on a great show of religiosity. The Pharisees received Christ's most stringent words because they were hypocrites, playing the part of spiritually alive people while actually being dead inside. They were all about externals, while Jesus never cared for package and performance and never will. He wants what's *real*: a heart abandoned in faith and trust. He wants you to trust Him to pilot the plane, to take you home.

Jesus said to the crowds and to his disciples, "The scribes and the Pharisees sit on Moses' seat, so do and observe whatever they tell you, but not the works they do. For they preach, but do not practice. They tie up heavy burdens, hard to bear, and lay them on people's shoulders, but they themselves are not willing to move them with their finger." (Matt. 23:1–4)

Living under the law is a weight too heavy to bear. And it's a weight we were never meant to bear. God intended the law to turn us back to Him, not to push us further into the sins of self-reliance and self-righteousness. He has never wanted us to act like we have everything together while we're empty and dead inside. That, however, is exactly what the rule-following, pedigree-proclaiming, performance-driven followers of the law were doing. Jesus exposed them.

Woe to you, scribes and Pharisees, hypocrites! For you clean the outside of the cup and the plate, but inside they are full of greed and self-indulgence. You blind Pharisee! First clean the inside of the cup and the plate, that the outside also may be clean. (vv. 25–26)

Just like you wouldn't trust a guy to fly a plane simply because he's got wings tattooed on his back and flying in his family bloodline, you wouldn't trust a blind guide. Yet that's precisely what following the law is like, and people continue to go down the road with the blind guide of the law. Why on earth would they do it?

The sad truth is that some people would rather *seem* than be. They'd rather look righteous on the outside—maybe showing up at every church event, maybe giving big donations to charity, maybe making a show of long prayers or "powerful" spiritual messages and music—than actually be holy. Modern-day Pharisees are people who might spend a whole lot of time curating their image on Facebook while only ever putting their face in God's book so they can answer Bible trivia and appear spiritually strong.

Trying to follow the path of the law naturally leads to spiritual pride and spiritual hiding. You have to look down on others in order to keep up appearances. You have to maintain the charade at all times. You also have to hide every sin. But when you're prideful and hiding, guess what else happens? Separation from God and your life's purpose.

The Bible tells us there are three major objectives for life on earth:

- ▶ Know God (John 17:3).
- ▶ Be known by Him (1 Cor. 8:3).
- ▶ Make Him known (1 Pet. 2:9).

The Pharisees got it all wrong. They wanted to know Scripture but not the God who inspired it. They wanted to be known by people and make themselves known. It was a recipe for disaster in Jesus's day, and it's a recipe for disaster now. To move from dying religion to a living relationship, we must follow the path of grace and the purposes for which we were designed.

I'm so grateful that others have gone before us down this road. Like the apostle Paul, we can say no to spiritual playacting and deadly self-reliance. Paul says these things are worthless, and he told the Philippian church,

> Indeed, I count everything as loss because of the surpassing worth of knowing Christ Jesus my Lord. For his sake I have suffered the loss of all things and count them as rubbish, in order that I may gain Christ and be found in him, not having a righteousness of my own that comes from the law, but that which comes through faith in Christ, the righteousness from God that depends on faith—that I may know him and the power of his resurrection, and may share his sufferings, becoming like him in his death, that by any means possible I may attain the resurrection from the dead. (Phil. 3:8–11)

The Greek word translated "rubbish" in verse 8 is *skybalon*. The literal translation is "dung."[1] In other words, you can try, try, try and do, do, do to get things right apart from God, but it'll all end up as doo-doo in the end . . . *skybalon*.

Knowing God is the path of grace, but it's also the reward. Knowing God is a treasure of such great value that everything else seems like *skybalon* in comparison. It's not another path of burdensome weight, like the path of the law. It's a journey full of greater joy and peace with each step forward. You can't know and experience it until you get into the plane with Jesus, though. The law will continue to flex its muscles and show you the how-to manual. You have to reject that offer. It's time to trust and step out in faith.

TRAVELING LIGHTLY

When I was twelve years old, I got a brilliant idea. *I'll show Mom and Dad what a great son I am. They'll be so proud of me. They'll never wonder again if it was worth it to have me.*

I set on a course of—I must say—pretty impressive house cleaning. I mean, I was washing windows till they sparkled. I mowed the lawn with putting-green precision. I went after the neglected stuff that was piled and hidden in various places.

After a few hours of this, Dad stopped me.

"What are you doing, son? You've been cleaning all day. This is weird."

Not exactly the reaction I had been hoping for.

"I just wanted to make you guys proud. I don't want you to think it's a waste to have me in the family."

"Rashawn, you're my son because you're my son. You don't have anything to prove."

You'd think I'd be happy to hear that. And I was. But I was also torn inside. I wanted to be noticed and appreciated for what I'd done. I wanted that to matter. I didn't realize until many years later that God was teaching me an important distinction between working *for* approval and working *from* it.

At twelve years old, I was working *for* my dad's smile. I wanted to impress him. I was trying to earn his appreciation and prove my value. But I didn't have to; I already had a position in the family, and working for attention only left me feeling grumpy and empty inside.

Everything changes when we know God the way Paul describes in Philippians 3, the "everything else is *skybalon* but You" way. When we know God in this way, we work *from* a place of peace. We have nothing to prove, and we don't try to. Everything we do becomes a gift with no strings attached, just like the gift of grace we've been given by Christ. We're not putting on a show, trying to impress by following the law. We're living like Jesus, serving and loving and being like Him, not so that others will notice but because we love our heavenly Father. We're looking for His and only His attention, confident that our highest reward will come on the day He says, "Well done, good and faithful servant" (Matt. 25:23).

To travel lightly on your journey with Jesus, ditch the list of dos and don'ts that rely on the law. Follow the leading of the Spirit instead. Checking off endless spiritual boxes—*Did I pray today? Did I read the Bible? Did I help someone in need? Did I do more good than bad? Did I (fill in the blank)?*—will only lead to dying religion, spiritual pride, and deadly self-reliance. Instead of living by a list, let God know you the way David did. He prayed,

> Search me, O God, and know my heart!
> Try me and know my thoughts!
> And see if there be any grievous way in me,
> and lead me in the way everlasting!
> (Ps. 139:23–24)

The thought of being known by God in this way unnerves a lot of people. Maybe that's why they'd rather stick with the lists and the laws. It feels vulnerable to be exposed to the gaze of Almighty God. And it is. But it's also the place of deepest security and peace a human can know. Grace is vulnerable, but it's also good. When you acknowledge to Jesus that you have nothing to prove and can't hide anything from Him (by the way, He already knows it all anyway), you'll be able to move forward lightly and freely with Him.

Some people fall into old sinful patterns because religion has failed them. *It's all too much*, they think. Others keep turning back to the same empty promises of religion, packaged in different ways. "If you pray *this* way, God will hear you." "If you follow *this* quiet-time plan, your problems will go away." "Do X, give Y, think Z, and you'll finally feel at peace with yourself." They believe following a formula will give them what they're seeking; instead it gives only dying religion.

It's often been said that religion is humankind's attempt to reach God, while relationship is God's gift to reach humankind. There's so much to chew on there. Stop trying to reach God on your own. That way sucks the life from your very soul. Instead, let God reach out to you. Live in relationship with Him. He is the way, the truth, and the life you are looking for.

Our heavenly Father didn't ask Jesus to come to earth so that He might be the founder of a new religion. Jesus came to set us free from the curse of sin: death. Why, then, would we give ourselves to religion that leaves us feeling exhausted and judged? Instead, let's look at ways we can cultivate our living relationship with Christ through knowing God and being known by Him.

TRAVELING WISELY

After you've said no to the lure of performance-driven religion and the lists of laws that burden people rather than setting them free, you have the chance to say yes to your living relationship with God. Because knowing God and being known by Him are the top two purposes of our lives, I've created the acronym K.N.O.W. to help us do so.

K Is for Kneeling

When you seek God on your knees, through prayer, you come in a position of humility and openness. This allows God room to work in your heart and cleanse you of anything that might separate you from Him. Habakkuk 1:13 reminds us that "[God's] eyes are too pure to look on evil; [He] cannot tolerate wrongdoing" (NIV). Before you can know God and be known by Him, you must welcome His redeeming work into your life. Praying helps us keep "short accounts" with God, which means we don't get too far from Him. Kneeling in prayer also keeps us from spiritual pride, which is a pathway to dying religion if ever there was one.

Jesus told a parable of two men who went up to the temple to pray. One was a Pharisee, a man everyone else believed to be super respectable and religious. The other was a tax collector, a man known for cheating and manipulating in any way possible to get ahead. Jesus's listeners certainly would have equated the words "tax collector" with "sinner." But Jesus, as He often did, flipped the script. He told the crowds and His disciples,

The Pharisee stood by himself and prayed: "God, I thank you that I am not like other people—robbers, evildoers, adulterers—or even like this tax collector. I fast twice a week and give a tenth of all I get." But the tax collector stood at a distance. He would not even look up to heaven, but beat his breast and said, "God, have mercy on me, a sinner." I tell you that this man, rather than the other, went home justified before God. For all those who exalt themselves will be humbled, and those who humble themselves will be exalted. (Luke 18:11–14 NIV)

When we kneel in prayer, acknowledging our sin and asking God to have mercy on us and help us, we draw closer to God. We know Him better. He can know us better because we are not posturing and pretending. And, as a beautiful benefit, we are exalted by Him in His ways and on His time frame.

N Is for Nurturing

Just as a flower cut from its stalk wilts and will eventually die, a soul cut off from God withers and moves toward death. That's why, if you want to know God and be known by Him, you must nurture your relationship with Him. How? By spending time with your Savior. You may remember from an earlier chapter that the Bible calls this *abiding*. You make yourself at home in God's heart and welcome Him to be at home in yours.

Often this nurturing can happen when you read His Word. It can also happen as you worship Him at church, in fellowship with other Christians. You can spend time with Him while you serve. Enjoying God in His creation or keeping a gratitude journal can also nurture your relationship with Him. You can cultivate your relationship with God by reading books like this one. Only remember to keep your eyes on Jesus while you read, not simply on tips and techniques for being a better person.

Consider using any creative gifts He's given you to express your appreciation or admiration for God. Music, visual arts, dance, calligraphy, quilting, graphic design, woodworking . . . the possibilities are endless for connecting with God through acts of creation. God, our Creator, made you a "subcreator." Think of it like this: God is the general contractor, and you're a subcontractor in His employ. When you create because He's made you a creator, you bring honor and glory to Him while you get to know Him better.

O Is for Offering

This one is quite simple. Offer your day to God. When you surrender your schedule to Him, He will work all things together to help you know Him and be known by Him. God can use the events of your day to point you back to Him. So often we relinquish control to the "tyranny of the urgent," to our social media feeds, to the people in our lives who clamor for our attention. Offering your schedule to God doesn't mean you ignore your responsibilities at work or in your family. In fact, staying closer to God in this way helps you grow as an employee, a parent or child, a friend, a church member. You know God and are known by Him when you surrender your day to Him.

W Is for Worshiping

"My heart says of you, 'Seek his face!' Your face, Lord, I will seek" (Ps. 27:8 NIV). The greatest thing you can do to journey as a Christian is FaceTime with God or, as the psalmist puts it, "Seek his face!" Unlike phone calls and text messages, FaceTime requires undivided attention. It's also planned and done with no other distractions. When we are too distracted to devote ourselves to the Messiah, we tend to send Him short, superficial, and self-centered messages. How sad would it be to refuse spending time *face-to-face* with the One who brings radiant joy to your face and fills your soul with an incomparable love?

Here's some good news: once we begin to know God more and are better known by Him, we cannot help but worship Him with all we are. It just spills out of us! Psalm 29 commands us: "Ascribe to the Lord glory and strength. Ascribe to the Lord the glory due his name; worship the Lord in the splendor of holiness" (vv. 1–2). We are invited to worship—to know and be known by—the Lord of glory, splendor, and holiness. It's an invitation to life everlasting instead of dead religion.

Kneel before God in humility, nurture your relationship, offer your schedule to Him, and worship Him as you know Him better. This is the way to cultivate an all-in, sold-out-for-Jesus lifestyle. That's the journey I'm on, and I pray you'll stay on the path with me.

TRAVELING TOGETHER

Spend some time talking with God or discussing the following with an accountability partner or small group.

- ► In your own words, what is the difference between religion and a relationship with God? Why is it important to make this distinction?

- ► Are you personally more tempted to spiritual pride and self-reliance or striving to please God by performing perfectly? How do these paths lead to dying religion rather than a living relationship with Christ?

- ► Think about a time you have felt most alive in Christ and closest to God your heavenly Father. To what do you attribute the vibrancy of your relationship during that season? How can identifying that help you move forward on your journey with Jesus?

- ► In which area of knowing God and being known by Him—kneeling before God in prayer, nurturing your relationship with Him, offering your schedule to Him, or allowing your knowledge to overflow in worship—do you want to grow? How can you start this very week?

POINTS TO PONDER AS YOU PROGRESS

Remember, legalism is trusting yourself, and it's dishonoring to God. Your life will be freer and fuller when you understand that . . .

You don't have to *prove yourself to God.*

You don't have to *prove yourself to people.*

You don't have to *prove yourself to yourself.*

Jesus already proved every point by paying the price. He perfected every flaw by dying a brutal death on the cross for you. But don't feel sorry for Jesus; He gave His life joyfully, in order to rescue you and redeem His relationship with you.

From Risk-Free Living to Radical Faith

My biggest fear, even now, is that I will hear Jesus' words and walk away.

DAVID PLATT, *Radical: Taking Back Your Faith from the American Dream*

THESE DAYS IT SEEMS EVERYONE wants to be an influencer. Recent studies revealed that Gen Z and Millennials, in particular, love the idea of monetizing social influence. Out of the two thousand participants in one survey, 86 percent said they would post sponsored content for money, and 54 percent would give up other career paths and become a full-time influencer if given the opportunity. Millennials cite flexibility and financial security as their top motivators for this, whereas Gen Z identifies "the

NO TURNING BACK

opportunity to make a difference in the world" as their chief inspiration. Most are willing to surrender privacy; some are willing to forfeit integrity. Almost a quarter of those surveyed would lie about loving a product as long as they were compensated.[1]

Digital influence certainly isn't the only desirable form of sway. In an op-ed piece for the *New York Times*, essayist Joseph Epstein revealed that a whopping 81 percent of surveyed Americans believed they "had a book in them" and felt they should write it. "Beyond the obvious motivation for wanting to write a book—hoping to win fame or fortune—my guess is that many people who feel they 'have a book in them' doubtless see writing it as a way of establishing their own significance," Epstein observed.[2] Bottom line: humans want influence. Imagine how many of these survey participants would jump, if given the chance, to be selected among their country's top five greatest people of all time and pen eighteen books, translated into sixty-five languages with well over ten million copies in print.

Of those, how many do you suppose would be willing to endure rejection, imprisonment, and bodily torture to secure this opportunity? Suddenly, you've got a lot less takers for this adventure. Such, however, was the radical, epic, and influential life of Dr. Richard Wurmbrand.

Orphaned at an early age and brought up in extreme poverty and bitterness during the difficult days of WWI Romania, Wurmbrand was of Jewish descent but grew up with a profound distrust of religion. An avowed atheist and student of Marxism at age fourteen, he viewed faith and its expressions as dangerous to humanity and society.

172

If there was a God, Wurmbrand believed, He would be "a master whom I should have to obey." At the same time, the lonely young man noted that he still "would have liked very much to know that a loving heart existed somewhere in the center of this universe. . . . I convinced myself that there was no God, but I was sad that such a God of love did not exist."[3]

In the meantime, in an isolated Romanian village, a devout Christian man prayed that God would allow him to share the gospel with one Jew. No Jews lived in his village, however, and he could not leave to seek one out, poor, old, and sick as he was. "Please bring a Jew to my village," this man prayed. "And I will speak to him of You." As Richard Wurmbrand remembers it, something irresistible and inexplicable drew him to that village. "Romania has twelve thousand villages, but I went to that one." Once he was there, that godly old man shared Christ with him, "not so much in words, but in flames of love fired by his prayers."[4] The fruit of this old man's radical prayer life was a radical conversion in young Richard Wurmbrand's life. The influence of these two men still echoes strongly some seventy years later.

After eagerly and joyfully training for the pastorate, Wurmbrand faithfully served Christ during the WWII Nazi regime. He and his wife endured beatings, multiple arrests, and false accusations that brought them before Nazi judges. "But these Nazi times had one great advantage. They taught us that physical beatings could be endured, and that the human spirit with God's help can survive horrible tortures."[5]

By the time one million Russian troops occupied Romania in 1944, bringing with them a communist party that would soon wrest power from the king of Romania and establish totalitarian rule, Wurmbrand had already lived a radical life for Jesus Christ. His epic testimony, however, had only just begun.

Wurmbrand recounted his experience at a parliament convened by the communist powers in his international bestselling book, *Tortured for Christ*. Four thousand spiritual leaders had gathered, and

> these men of God chose Joseph Stalin as honorary president of this congress. At the same time, he was president of the World Movement of the Godless and a mass murderer of Christians. One after another, bishops and pastors arose and declared that communism and Christianity are fundamentally the same and could coexist. [They] said words of praise toward communism and assured the new government of the loyalty of the Church.[6]

Wurmbrand's wife, Sabina, leaned over and whispered to him, "Stand up and wash away this shame from the face of Christ! They are spitting in His face."

"If I do so, you lose your husband," Wurmbrand replied.

Her response: "I don't wish to have a coward as a husband."

That day, Wurmbrand arose and spoke, praising not the communists but Jesus Christ, affirming that his own and the entire church's loyalty was due first to God. Because the congress's speeches were broadcast across the whole country, all Romanians could hear the message of Christ proclaimed from the rostrum of the communist parliament. Afterward, Wurmbrand remembered, "I had to pay for this, but it was worthwhile."[7]

Pay he certainly did. With fourteen years of his life. With solitary confinement in dank prisons. With regular near-death beatings. With four broken vertebrae and other bones, cruel carvings on his skin, and permanent scars from vicious burns. He also witnessed the suffering of fellow Christians tortured around him, some of them beaten, burned, starved, or frozen to death. Though he wrote eighteen books, to his dying day he refused to detail every atrocity he experienced; the brutality was too great.

Eight years into his imprisonment, Wurmbrand was released for a brief time. Though many begged him to leave Romania and protect himself, Wurmbrand continued to preach the gospel. When he was apprehended by the communist secret police once again, he knew what awaited him in prison. He did not want to return to the savage horrors he had already endured for eight years, but God carried him through another six-plus years of confinement and brutality.

After his release, Wurmbrand wrote,

One great lesson arose from all the beatings, tortures and butchery of the Communists: that the spirit is master of the body. We felt the torture, but it often seemed as something distant and far removed from the spirit which was lost in the glory of Christ and His presence with us.[8]

He endured by the strength and courage of Emmanuel—God with him.

In the years after his imprisonment, Wurmbrand went back to his work with the underground church in Romania. And while he faced a constant threat of arrest, Wurmbrand would have stayed there forever, had the Romanian church leaders not commissioned him to emigrate to the West and publicize the plight of the persecuted Christians under communist rule.

The Wurmbrands thus devoted the remainder of their lives to helping those persecuted for their faith in Jesus Christ. Richard founded an international organization that, to this day, provides aid to Christians around the world who face daily persecution, not just under communism but under any anti-Christian regime. The influence of his life is staggering. Well over ten million people have read his books, which have been translated into sixty-five languages. Romania has named Richard Wurmbrand among its top five most important people of all time.

Wurmbrand could have played it safe. He could have "played nice" with the communist government, not giving in to them, per se, but not defending Christ either. Most of the other pastors did this; they believed the risk was too great. Richard and Sabine, however, cared less about risk than they did about what's right. They lived radically for their Lord and Savior, who lived and died radically for them.

Most of us will never be asked to face what Dr. Richard Wurmbrand and his family did. I praise God for that. That said, Jesus asks every single one us to decide whether we'll live risk-free or radically. The amount of influence we'll have in eternity is directly related to that choice.

How much would you sacrifice for your Savior? Are you willing to talk to your family members or coworkers about the Jesus who died for you? Are you willing to go places and do things for His sake that other people might view as risky? Things like giving generously and sacrificially, reaching those that others would reject, and going when you feel like staying?

My friend, it's highly unlikely we'll ever face imprisonment or death because of our faith. Reading a story like Wurmbrand's does make me question how radically I'm really living for my Lord, though. A risk-free life and a no-turning-back life simply cannot coexist. You must choose one or the other. If you genuinely want to live for Jesus, if you want influence that lasts beyond a social media post or a viral video, there are risks involved. But, oh, how very worth it Jesus is!

WHERE WE'VE COME FROM

Let's just put all the cards on the table right now: humans like comfort. C'mon. You know it's true. No one intentionally buys an uncomfortable couch or bed. You may endure one given to you for free, but you aren't likely to plunk down your hard-earned coin for furniture that makes you grumpy. And no one I know gets excited that uncomfortable conversations may come up around the family dinner table during the holidays; most people would gladly and quickly opt out of that if they could. "Roughing it" appeals to very few. Risk-taking may interest more people, but only if they get something really cool with it: a major adrenaline rush, street cred, or some other kind of benefit. People like to be comfortable.

If we're really honest, we like to be comfortable in our faith too. We don't like to be at a church where we don't know the songs, or where the lighting or stage dynamics feel unfamiliar to us. How "they" do the offering or the fellowship time may seem awkward, especially if we're used to something different. We love hearing about Jesus's love for us in a sermon, but it's discomforting to hear that Jesus might want us to extend that love to other people such as ex-convicts, those on the other side of the political spectrum, that family member who owes us money (a lot of money), or a member of *that* religion, race, or community.

Right now, in the United States of America—where I live—it's easier to live a risk-free Christianity than it is almost anywhere else. I don't face bodily persecution. I may get some hate on social media if I post about my faith, but I'm not facing a prison sentence anytime soon. I also don't have to serve at my church. There's enough money to hire staff and plenty of other volunteers to keep me comfortable and the ministries running. I don't have to share the gospel with anyone; I can just buy them a book, a Bible, or a digital resource that will tell them all about Jesus while I sit at home in my comfortable chair with my comfortable blanket, binge-watching mindless television. This is the life!

Or is it?

Is this what I was made for?

Is comfort the highest goal?

No way, Jose!

Why am I—along with millions of others—attracted to superhero stories? Because going where no one else wants to go and rescuing people no one else can is epic. And I think you and I were made for an *epic* life, not a comfortable one.

Don't get me wrong; comfort is awesome. I'm enjoying a warm home and a full belly while I write this. Comfort isn't the only thing worth living for though. I learned this some years ago after I had been invited to a Christian influencer retreat in Estes Park, Colorado.

If you know nothing about Estes Park, just picture the most gorgeous natural surroundings with wildlife roaming in and out of view and breathtaking sunrises and sunsets over the Rocky Mountains. Yeah. That kind of fabulous. I can't emphasize enough how much I looked forward to this retreat. Other conference speakers, worship leaders, and influencers from around the country would gather to worship, pray, and strategize together. I was lit and ready.

Then I got a call from a buddy of mine, Shorty. I'd met Shorty while serving as a prison guard. If you read my first book, *Start Where You Are*, he's the inmate who threw his urine on me before he surrendered his life to Jesus (you seriously have to read that story sometime).

Shorty called to ask me to preach at a gang outreach that same weekend. I felt torn, and the two parts of me kept going back and forth: Should I hang around saints or sinners, God's people or gang members, conference speakers and worship leaders or Crips and Bloods?

"Rashawn, leave the ninety-nine and come after the one, man. You gotta do this," Shorty pleaded. I knew crime had been spiking in our city. I knew Shorty needed help. I knew the East Side was a dangerous place but one in which God could do amazing things.

And I went to Colorado anyway.

I chose the comfortable path. And I regret it to this day.

After the retreat, I felt high on Christ. But the spiritual buzz of the weekend eventually wore off. I started to wonder whether I had made the right decision. I called Shorty and told him God had placed a strong burden on my heart. "Can I please get involved with whatever you're doing?"

He laughed at me.

But then he continued, "Rashawn, your party out in Colorado stopped; but there ain't no party like a Holy Ghost party, 'cause a Holy Ghost party don't stop. We've got so much else we can do for the gospel."

The day I heard that from Shorty, I took a step away from risk-free Christianity and toward a life of radical faith. I think God made the contrast between the two paths so distinct because He didn't want me to miss the lesson. Risk-free Christianity, comfortable Christianity, doesn't last. You keep having to ward off things that make you uncomfortable—you know, like people's needs. When you're living radically for Christ, however, you don't have to hide, even from things that make you squirm. Now, this doesn't mean it's all tough with no comfort from that point forward, thank God. Instead, it's a life open to possibility—a potentially epic life.

If where we've been is wanting only comfort, where do we head once we've decided to live a radical life for our radical Savior?

WHERE WE'RE HEADED

The simplest way for me to describe where we're headed takes us back to a story I related in the introduction. Do you remember the tribesman who surrendered his life rather than deny Jesus? He died with these words on his lips: "The world behind me, the cross before me . . . no turning back, no turning back." Where we've been is focused on comfort. Where we're headed is focused on *surrender*. Surrender is the key to a radical life.

Does surrender automatically mean you'll be martyred for your faith? Lose all your money? Never be physically comfortable again? No. It doesn't always mean that. But what if it did? Do you even *want* to develop the kind of resilience that would enable you to live as radically as Dr. Richard Wurmbrand in Romania or the thousands of Middle Eastern Christians who gave everything rather than be counted with ISIS? If you and I don't even want this kind of radical faith, we'll never pursue a radical life.

So let me ask you again: Do you *want* this?

We've already established that most people in today's culture want to influence others. Whether their motivations are pure—to change and help the world—or more mercenary—to have a flexible schedule and monetary success—people want to have influence. The amazing truth is that God made us to do so. Jesus tells us this in John 15:16: "I chose you and appointed you so that you might go and bear fruit—fruit that will last" (NIV). What you do, who you are, is supposed to be influential through eternity; it's supposed to last. Would you rather have influence for a moment or influence for eternity?

Put that simply, it's a no-brainer, isn't it? Unfortunately, we don't often get to make decisions in this kind of simplistic format. In the real world, the choice to keep the course often appears far more difficult. Surrender isn't always easy. In some ways, however, it is simple. Surrender is waking up every day and praying, as Jesus did on the Mount of Olives, "Not my will, but yours, be done" (Luke 22:42).

This is where we're headed: surrendering to the will of Christ.

I praise God that walking with faith, into His will, means the kind of life, joy, peace, and love that can never be taken away. "The eternal God is your refuge, and his everlasting arms are under you. He drives out the enemy before you" (Deut. 33:27 NLT). Did you catch the words *eternal* and *everlasting* there? God wants us to know—without a shadow of a doubt—that His promises are forever promises.

That's why we can claim, with the apostle Paul, "But one thing I do: forgetting what lies behind and straining forward to what lies ahead, I press on toward the goal for the prize of the upward call of God in Christ Jesus" (Phil. 3:13–14). These verses exemplify what I long for you to do. Surrender what's behind so you can live radically today . . . and forever.

The places God takes us aren't always safe, because God Himself isn't safe—at least the way the world defines it. Ask a few of our friends from the Bible. What do we do when confronted with this reality? Like Adam, we sometimes hide from God. Like Peter, we may deny Him. Like Jonah, we often run in the opposite direction. Our loving heavenly Father is a radical God who radically pursues us, even when we're afraid, even when we start to shrink back. Just look what He did to save us! Can you get any more radical than the rescue mission of redemption Jesus fulfilled through His death and resurrection?

There is no greater adventure than following our radical Savior. This epic journey, Jesus tells us, will be full of grace, joy, and love. It will also involve denying ourselves, picking up our cross, and following Him. Like Jonah, we are called to Nineveh; like Paul, we are called to the nations; or perhaps, like the Samaritan woman at the well, we are called no farther than our own hometown, which is also full of people who desperately need the hope of Christ.

For years, I've heard the Christian cliché "The safest place in the world is in the center of God's will." Try telling that to Daniel in the lion's den or Esther in King Xerxes's palace or Shadrach, Meshach, and Abednego in the fiery furnace. Or Dr. Wurmbrand being beaten in a Romanian prison. Were these followers of Christ "safe" in the way the world understands it? *Hardly!*

I think these kinds of glib clichés, along with the whole "your best life now" movement, have done a great deal of damage to the body of Christ. If we're called to a life that is resilient and radical, that leaves our past behind and strains toward what is ahead, that picks up our cross daily—which is precisely what we are called to—how can we live our "best" life now? Safety as the world perceives it isn't what we're promised. Being held in the everlasting arms, eternally safe, is. And this is a covenant worth every possible earthly risk. This is the reward that never fails or changes.

Perhaps our battle cry should be "Live your best life *later*." Whether you choose to live this way or not, heaven is your true home. You were never meant to dwell here, only journey from here to the place of eternal promise and spiritual reward, in the everlasting arms of Jesus. Surrendering to Him may not be "safe," but it's so good. Forever good. Surrendering in a radical way also enables you to face the sufferings of today with courage and hope.

Just as Paul encouraged the Corinthian church, he also encourages you and me:

> Do not lose heart. Though our outer self is wasting away, our inner self is being renewed day by day. For this light momentary affliction is preparing for us an eternal weight of glory beyond all comparison, as we look not to the things that are seen but to the things that are unseen. For the things that are seen are transient, but the things that are unseen are eternal. (2 Cor. 4:16–18)

The world behind me, the cross before me . . . no turning back, no turning back.

TRAVELING LIGHTLY

I travel a lot for my work. I love hopping on a plane, whether it be to share the gospel in Philadelphia or the Philippines. I pack my bags and head to the airport, knowing an adventure awaits. This kind of life isn't for everyone, but it's perfect for me.

Heading out on a mission trip is a very different experience than preparing for a family vacation. If I'm taking a road trip with Denisse and the kids, we pack everything and the kitchen sink to make sure our toddlers are happy and comfortable. We've got the snacks they love, the Disney movies, and their favorite clothes and blankies. The goal of a family vacation is *fun*, and we want to make sure we've got everything that will make fun possible. We've also made plans that help us maximize fun and minimize stress. I'm usually eager to get to our destination. Once I get there, I'm considered a tourist, defined by the dictionary as "a person traveling, especially for pleasure."[9]

It occurs to me that a lot of Christians live more like tourists than they do like travelers on the road of faith. They're looking for pleasure and comfort; they want the love and grace and peace of Christ. "I'll pass on the suffering, thank you very much," a tourist might say. In contrast, a Christian traveler embraces the risky, radical life of faith. A traveler embarks on a journey, not a vacation. A Christian traveler is a sojourner, "a person who lives or stays temporarily in a place."[10] We are only temporarily here on earth. Eternity is our true destination. For believers, heaven is home. The motivations of a Christian tourist and a traveler are very different; ultimately they boil down to fun versus faithfulness. Not that journeying with Jesus isn't a blast too. It's just that fun and comfort are no longer our main motivations.

My grandma used to describe my grandpa with words the Motown Temptations sang: "Papa was a rolling stone; wherever he laid his hat was his home." My grandpa was an old-school nomad, the kind of guy who would literally hop on a train with only his hat and a small bag. He traveled lightly because the journey was more important to him than making sure he had everything to secure his creature comforts.

Though I'm not endorsing a nomadic lifestyle, here's what I do endorse: a "take nothing with you" lifestyle.

Jesus commanded this of His disciples in Luke 9:3. "Take nothing for the journey," He told them, "no staff, no bag, no bread, no money, no extra shirt" (NIV). To me, that sounds like nothing *except faith in Him*, which is the only thing that pleases God (see Heb. 11:6). Here's why I am advocating a Christian traveler mentality rather than a tourist one: traveling lightly is the mark of a pilgrim ready to live radically for Jesus Christ and Him alone.

A radical life trusts in

Jesus as *protector*. Not a pistol.

Jesus as *guide*. Not a GPS.

Jesus as *provider*. Not a bank account.

Jesus as *healer*. Not a bottle of medicine.

Jesus as *teacher*. Not Google or YouTube.

I urge you, as God commands in Hebrews 12, to

lay aside every weight, and sin which clings so closely, and . . . run with endurance the race that is set before us, looking to Jesus, the founder and perfecter of our faith, who for the joy that was set before him endured the cross, despising the shame, and is seated at the right hand of the throne of God. (vv. 1–2)

Consider the radical life of Jesus, who endured the utmost suffering. He did it *for* something . . . and I'm not only speaking of the forgiveness of our sins. Look back at those verses and take note of why Jesus endured: for *joy.* Not the kind of joy that fades, like memories or old-school photographs from vacations past, but eternal joy, the kind of joy that allows us to look shame square in the face and say, "Not today, Satan."

Traveling lightly includes leaving your past behind. To live it up in Christ, you've got to *burn it up* and *give it up.*

Burn up your past. You may have heard the saying "Don't burn the bridges you may have to cross later." That may be true of some things, but with regard to our former way of living, God calls us to become holy arsonists. Light it up! Choose to travel lightly by burning the bridges to your old ways.

Giving up your fears and your ego also allows you to travel lightly. Give it up! Go places no one else wants to go, whether that means Nigeria or your neighbor's house. It's not about the destination with God. It's about the surrender, the obedience, the joy set before you, the joy that only comes when you lay everything down, just like Jesus did. Christians weren't meant to stay safe in church buildings, cozy Christian circles, book clubs, private social media groups, and so on. We are the church, a city on a hill. We have been called to shine radically for Christ. Never forget the command of God in Matthew 5:16: "Let your light shine before others, so that they may see your good works and give glory to your Father who is in heaven." We have been lit by the flaming torch of God's love to light up a dark and dying world.

Are we light takers? Or light makers?

A Christian tourist is all about what they're getting out of church. A Christian traveler is focused on *giving*. Christian tourists move through life heavily, toting around the things and people and memories that make them feel safe and comfortable. Christian travelers burn up the past, give up fear, lay down ego, and surrender their will for God's will . . . so that they can be "salt and light" in the world (see vv. 13–16). Both salt and light have healing properties. Both purify things. And I'll also add that life would be a whole lot less enjoyable without salt and light. Being a radical Christian isn't about being serious and intense all the time. There are certainly times for that, but we're also called to flavor life—to bring out its very best—like salt does food and stars do the blackest night (see Phil. 2:15).

Living radically means traveling lightly. It also means traveling wisely.

TRAVELING WISELY

A radical life requires that we not just remember who we are (and who we are not) but believe it. Go back and reread the chapters on identity and kinship if you need reminders of who you truly are. You are a child of God, lavishly loved by your Father, accepted completely and without reservation . . . forever. A radical life also requires rediscovering the sacred risks that come with belonging to Him. This means abandoning the illusion of safety and embracing your omnipotent, omniscient, limitless God, who is infinite in wisdom, knowledge, and understanding. A radical life is a life fully dependent on our risen Savior.

Some live radically for a season. They give sacrificially, go sacrificially, serve sacrificially. Then they tire out. Living a radical *life* for Christ, not merely for a season but forever, is like running a marathon rather than a hundred-meter dash. As Eugene Peterson puts it, a radical life is a "long obedience in the same direction."[11] It takes cultivating humility, nurturing a heart eager to surrender to God each and every day, and becoming rooted and grounded in God. "For this reason I bow my knees before the Father," just like Paul did on behalf of the Ephesians (Eph. 3:14). Right this moment, I pray

that according to the riches of his glory he may grant you to be strengthened with power through his Spirit in your inner being, so that Christ may dwell in your hearts through faith—that you, being rooted and grounded in love, may have strength to comprehend with all the saints what is the breadth and length and height and depth, and to know the love of Christ that surpasses knowledge, that you may be filled with all the fullness of God.

Now to him who is able to do far more abundantly than all that we ask or think, according to the power at work within us, to him be glory in the church and in Christ Jesus throughout all generations, forever and ever. Amen. (vv. 16–21)

It becomes less and less desirable to sin when we've tasted and seen the love that surpasses knowledge, when we're filled with all the fullness of God, when we see that He really, truly can do far more abundantly than all we can ask for or imagine. Traveling wisely means being rooted and grounded in this way.

Let's look at a couple practical ways to travel wisely on the road to radical faith in Jesus. May these equip you to lay down what burdens you have and pick up what will give you strength for the journey.

Focus on the Reward of Heaven

Obedience for obedience's sake can be noble, but we don't have to simply grit our teeth and suck it up to live a radical life of faith. We are promised a prize, a radical reward, so dwell on the promises of eternity: no more tears, no more pain, the celebration of the ages at the wedding feast of the Lamb, eternal joy and security. This is worth living for. Meditate on the Scriptures that provide pictures of what will be, like Isaiah 65:17; Revelation 7:13–17; John 14:2–4; Isaiah 25:8–12; and Revelation 21:4–8. When you focus on what's in store for you in the everlasting arms of Jesus, living radically will become more and more possible.

Anchor Yourself with Hope

The book of Hebrews tells us that hope is "a sure and steadfast anchor of the soul" (6:19), and this is because God is our hope. Hope is found in the unchangeable nature of our Lord. Don't lose hope, my friend. When the storms of suffering come into our lives, the enemy attacks our hope. He makes walking away from God seem desirable and conceals its dangers. That's exactly when being anchored in hope secures us.

It's tough to drop anchor from a ship while it's being tossed on stormy seas, but a ship that was anchored before the storm can withstand the wind and waves. In addition, consider this: living radically for Jesus would be foolish if it only pertained to our hopes for the here and now. First Corinthians 15:19 states it bluntly: "If in Christ we have hope in this life only, we are of all people most to be pitied." I praise God that our hope "does not put us to shame," as Romans 5:5 promises, "because God's love has been poured into our hearts through the Holy Spirit who has been given to us." Amen and amen.

Examine Your Life Frequently

Chances are, you look at yourself in a mirror every day. At the very least, you want to make sure you don't have something stuck in your teeth or something undone that should be done; it only takes one time going out with your zipper down to make you leery of leaving the house without at least a quick glance at your appearance. In our self-obsessed culture, most people spend a lot of time gazing at themselves. (Oh, wait! Let me stop writing for a sec and take a selfie. Ha!) They not only capture the best images of themselves but also go back and gaze at their own photos over and over again, as likes and comments post. *I've been guilty of this!*

How often do we examine our spiritual reflections, though? In my opinion, not nearly enough. It can feel devastating to look at my spiritual self and see how many areas of life I haven't surrendered completely to God. How about in my career, my family, my comfort? Thank God that "there is therefore now no condemnation for those who are in Christ Jesus" (Rom. 8:1).

Spiritual examination isn't about feeling terrible about what you have or haven't done. It's about what you and I do once we see our own reflection. Will we remain in the same place? If we see areas of our lives that aren't radically given to Jesus and still choose *not* to surrender, that's when we start turning back to risk-free Christianity. It's dangerous to examine yourself because you'll see areas in which Jesus would like you to journey higher up and further in with Him, but "let us not grow weary of doing good, for in due season we will reap, if we do not give up" (Gal. 6:9). We will reap a great reward for our radical faith; let's run after the eternal prize.

Pick Up Your Cross

We've already emphasized in this book that picking up our cross is a direct command of Jesus. This is the mantle of faith that produces radical fire in our lives. Very few pick up the cross. Some people study it. Many ignore it. Some acknowledge it, applaud it, or are impressed by it. These are safe options. Actually picking up your cross, though, is radical, right, and eternally rewarded by our God.

Double Up

Pray that God will increase your knowledge and fear of Him. When we view God correctly, complacency and comfort can't tempt us. Radical obedience to and radical love for Jesus become so much easier when we know how incredibly big, how incredibly great, how wonderfully gracious and merciful our God is. Safety becomes less of a deal when we know Him. The fear of others fades when we gaze at the heart of the Holy One. Ask God to double up your faith so you can double down on obedience . . . radical obedience.

I'LL LEAVE YOU, brothers and sisters, with one more scriptural prayer. As I write this,

> I do not cease to give thanks for you, remembering you in my prayers, that the God of our Lord Jesus Christ, the Father of glory, may give you the Spirit of wisdom and of revelation in the knowledge of him, having the eyes of your hearts enlightened, that you may know what is the hope to which he has called you, what are the riches of his glorious inheritance in the saints, and what is the immeasurable greatness of his power toward us who believe, according to the working of his great might that he worked in Christ when he raised him from the dead and seated him at his right hand in the heavenly places, far above all rule and authority and power and dominion, and above every name that is named, not only in this age but also in the one to come. And he put all things under his feet and gave him as head over all things to the church, which is his body, the fullness of him who fills all in all. (Eph. 1:16–23)

TRAVELING TOGETHER

Spend some time talking with God or discussing the following with an accountability partner or small group.

- In what ways have you wanted to influence others? What do you think about the kind of influence Dr. Richard Wurmbrand earned through his radical faith?

- How does the desire for comfort impact your faith? Is it easy or difficult for you to pray, like Jesus did before His death, "Not my will, but Yours, be done"?

- In what ways do Christian tourists and Christian travelers differ? Which currently describes your life of faith? What changes, if any, might the Holy Spirit be calling you to make?

- Read some or all of these verses that highlight our hope in heaven: Isaiah 65:17; Revelation 7:13–17; John 14:2–4; Isaiah 25:8–12; and Revelation 21:4–8. What excites you most about the reward awaiting you? How does this encourage you to abandon risk-free Christianity and pursue radical faith?

POINTS TO PONDER AS YOU PROGRESS

Let's finish with a note to Christians from Jan Hus, a vibrant follower of Jesus, who was martyred in the summer of 1415: "Faithful Christian, seek the truth, listen to the truth, learn the truth, love the truth, tell the truth, defend the truth even to death."[12]

Afterthought

YOUR BATTLE CRY—NO TURNING BACK!

Dark clouds bring waters, when the bright bring
none.

JOHN BUNYAN, *The Pilgrim's Progress*

WHEN I BEGAN WRITING THIS BOOK, I conducted an informal survey on my social media platforms, asking people to respond to the following question: "In your opinion, what are the main reasons some turn away from God?" Within ten minutes, I had thirty individual answers. After a few hours, over two hundred responses flooded my feed. People told their stories and opened their hearts in powerful ways. For some, this appeared to be an intellectual or theological exercise; for others, it was an agonizing reminder of their own wanderings.

I read my friends' responses with both understanding and sorrow. I resonated deeply with some of the heartache shared online. I understand how difficult it is to face pain we can't control and don't want. I grieved reading the stories of those whose experiences I hadn't shared and couldn't fully understand. What I could grasp, through every post, was how difficult it can be for my brothers and sisters in Christ to stay the course in faithful obedience and love, especially when faced with disappointment, disillusionment, doubt, and death.

People posted about trying to hold on to Jesus after the unexpected death of a loved one. The untimely loss of a child weighed heavily on some. Financial struggles burdened others. One commenter observed that seeing nonbelievers prosper while she felt she was barely getting by tempted her to walk away from her faith. Many others cited years of unanswered prayers as another primary reason Christians consider returning to their old ways. Lastly, one of the most common answers I received was that people tend to lose their desire and commitment to finish their journey with Christ because of hypocritical Christian leaders (e.g. celeb pastors in moral failure) and/or "church hurt" caused by being wounded by a brother or sister in Christ.

The most difficult answers for me to process were those that involved willful sin—perhaps because I didn't like what they said about me. Posters noted that selfishness, pride, busyness, unforgiveness, rejecting accountability, and living in lies rather than truth are major reasons people drift away from God. Ouch. Those hit close to home. Perhaps you've heard the old saying "Backsliding begins with dusty Bibles." The Bible is not just a valuable resource but the vital source for staying the course.

There were also mentions of neglecting God's Word and prayer, hanging around with worldly people, not investing in relationships with more mature believers, and laziness as causes of wandering. Yep; I know all about those.

What's the bottom line here? We get why people fall. We see the reasons all around us. There's no real mystery here. The enemy often makes it seem like it happens in a moment, but the reality is we see people—sometimes ourselves—surrendering to sin in little ways every day. I don't want to live like that, do you? Wanting to stay the course with Jesus motivated me to write this book. I pray reading it has challenged, changed, and motivated you too.

Right now, we need one another more than ever. We need to remind each other to live and die with the battle cry on our lips: no turning back.

THE BEGINNING AND THE END

We began this book by introducing the idea that each believer journeys through life as a pilgrim with Jesus. As we've seen, the Bible is full of references and metaphors related to this theme. As Christians in the twenty-first century, we also have access to hundreds of years of amazing books that have been written about the pilgrimage to our heavenly home.

Among the most famous of these is John Bunyan's 1678 classic, *The Pilgrim's Progress from This World, to That Which Is to Come*. Widely regarded as one of the most influential religious texts of all time, *Pilgrim's Progress* is the allegorical tale of a man, named Christian, who is born in the City of

Destruction and makes his way through trials and triumphs to the Celestial City. This journey corresponds to our own pilgrimage away from sin and toward our heavenly home with Jesus.

Along the way, Christian meets a variety of friends and foes. Each interaction teaches a lesson about the life of faith. Christian meets Giant Despair, who lives in Doubting Castle, torturing travelers in his dungeon and eventually blinding them. He encounters Talkative, who has much to say about faith but nothing to show for his many words; Talkative displays the hypocrisy and pride of knowing about God but never knowing Him personally. Christian also comes across the sniveling character Shame, who shadows travelers while hissing in their ears, trying to convince them the life of faith is only for the weak and foolish. As you can see, Christian meets personifications of many of the reasons people get distracted on the road to everlasting life.

Bunyan also penned a sequel to *Pilgrim's Progress*, simply called *Part II*. This story follows Christian's wife, Christiana, and their four sons, who eventually follow their husband-father on the way after initially rejecting him and the message of truth. Like Christian, Christiana encounters fiends and friends as she journeys in faith. In one such encounter, she meets a man "who couldn't look any way but down and in his hand he held a muck-rake. One stood above the man's head holding a celestial crown and he offered him that crown for his muck-rake. But the man didn't look up or regard the one holding the crown in any way. Instead, he only raked bits of straw, small sticks, and dust from the floor."[1]

Lest we miss the lesson of this muck-raker, Bunyan explains his predicament through the character named Interpreter.

> [Interpreter said,] "It is to show that heaven is nothing but a fable to some people, and that things here in this world are considered important to them. Now, when you saw that the man with the rake could only look down, it was to let you see that when earthly things hold power over men's minds, they completely carry their hearts away from God."
>
> Then Christiana said, "Oh, deliver me from this muck-rake."[2]

Amen, Lord. Please deliver us all from getting caught up in the muck of this life!

Don't focus on straw and dust when the crown of life awaits you. Heaven is not a fable. It's my home and yours, if you have received God's mercy through Jesus Christ. You cannot lose focus. Remember, Jesus is the path and the prize. Many people believe that, if they have completely surrendered to the Savior, they have gone the whole way. However, there is a difference between coming to Jesus (the Way) and going on in the way.

As we travel, we may experience loneliness. Embracing our faith journey can be challenging because, at the end of the day, we can only walk our own pilgrimage. Like I did, you may lose some friends in your walk with Jesus. *Beloved, don't fret.* No matter how much you've loved them or how long you've known them, you can't let people influence you to sin. Remember who your First Love is. This is why we must cultivate godly relationships to sustain us. As we close this book, think about people you can walk with as you and they follow Christ—God-fearing people who will encourage you to stay close to Jesus as you journey in faith.

Feeling lost along the way is also common. But remember, we walk by faith and not by feelings. That's when faith pushes back against the uppercuts of uncertainty and the jabs of jadedness. Pain, too, is a frequent companion on the pilgrimage, keeping us dependent on Christ and humble on our journey. Pain exposes our pride and purifies our hearts; it can also compel us to humbly cling to God's promises and press into His presence. Relying on God as our refuge and remaining hopeful in His sovereign plan are essential for the walk of faith.

Whether you are closer to the beginning of your journey with Jesus or the end, reflection is also an important component of your faith. Before you shut this book, deliberately decide that you will take time to see and savor the transforming power of the Holy Spirit who dwells inside you.

As we thank Him and allow Him to remind us of who we are in Christ—and of His power that we carry as we embrace the truth of our identity and become overwhelmingly excited about who we are becoming—our journey becomes increasingly joyful even when difficulties come. Amen!

PARTING GIFTS

You've come so far, and I'm privileged to have joined you for this part of your pilgrimage. *No turning back!* I'd like to close our time together with a few simple but practical ways to move forward and to bless you with the following collection of prayers and thoughts.

> ► *May you learn the infinite value of patience.* Never forget that growing in grace is slow-paced. It takes time. You've taken some stunning steps while reading this book. Well done. Your journey will continue, and patience will be needed. If we want to conform to the image of the perfect One, Jesus Christ, we must both exercise patience and understand God's patience with us. You and I will be pursing holiness the rest of our lives, as we await the day we will be glorified and welcomed home and will see our Savior face-to-face. Don't lose heart; instead, practice patiently.

> ► *May you travel in good company.* Pilgrims grow as they go together. You will become like those you spend the most time with, so choose your traveling companions wisely. I love these words from Jonathan Edwards's sermon "The Christian Pilgrim":

>> Let them go united and not fall out by the way, which would be to hinder one another, but use all means they can to help each other up hill. This would ensure a more successful traveling and a more joyful meeting at their Father's house in glory.[3]

> Find people who will help you uphill, and the journey will be more joyful.

> ► *May you learn the power of godly passion.* A pilgrim's heart ponders what Christ passionately pursues. If

your focus is on the world, so will your passions be. May you never be satisfied with anything less than God. We've seen throughout this book that true pilgrims have a passion for Christ and Him alone. They understand even the finest of things in this world are mere shadows; God is the true substance of our enjoyment. These things are scattered rays; God is the sun. These things are muddy puddles; God is the river of living water. Jesus says:

> Do not lay up for yourselves treasures on earth, where moth and rust destroy and where thieves break in and steal; but lay up for yourselves treasures in heaven, where neither moth nor rust destroys and where thieves do not break in and steal. (Matt. 6:19–20)

May your treasure and your heart be found in Christ, the Everlasting One.

▶ *May you always cultivate faith in God's promises.* Pilgrims move toward the promised land because they know the Promised One. God has promised the crown of life for those who faithfully endure (see Rev. 2:10). We are called to persevere until the end. May you have power to resist lies and replace them with the truth of God's promises, found in His Word. The great prize of heaven is dwelling with God Himself. There are many wonderful aspects of heaven described in Scripture: deliverance from all pain and suffering, resolution to all problems, being with loved ones who died before us, and the glories of golden streets and heavenly feasts. I can't wait! None of these phenomenal things, however, can compare to being in the presence of God, our Promised Redeemer. Imagine one thousand years from now: you're in heaven, surrounded by beauty that surpasses any splendor ever experienced on earth. Imagine the perfection of your glorified body and your heavenly home. How grateful do you imagine you'll be that you stayed the course with Jesus? It boggles and blows the mind, doesn't it? I pray that you and I might bring that kind of expectant hope in the promises of God to our lives right now.

▶ *May you remember—until the very end—that you are never alone.* We've come to the close of a remarkable segment of our life journey, my friend. I'm your companion on the journey going forward too. You can connect with me online @RashawnCopeland or @ImSoBlessedDaily. My team and I pray with and for those who submit prayer requests, so if you feel burdened, please reach out. Far, far more importantly, remember that God will never leave you nor forsake you. I won't always be there to reply to a comment or text, but your heavenly Father is closer than a breath away. May you close this book with these words ringing in your mind: "God has said, 'I will never fail you. I will never abandon you'" (Heb. 13:5 NLT).

The cross before us, the world behind us.

No turning back, no turning back.

Acknowledgments

FIRST OF ALL, thank you to Jesus for bringing life from death, beauty from ashes, and hope from despair and for making impossible things possible.

I am grateful for you, readers. Thank you for reading these words. I spent hours praying over this work and tapping out these words on my laptop (at times with a face full of tears). I was afraid, fearful, and painfully dreaded revisiting my past, but the love you've shown and the lives you live have helped carry me through some of my toughest days. Thank you!

Shawn, Tanda, Hayden, I love you guys so much. I've been able to watch Christ in you champion one of the greatest tragedies I've ever watched someone walk through. After losing everything in one night, including your daughter Berklee, in a home explosion in October 2020, you guys remained steadfast in the mercy and love of Christ. There are no words I could ever say that will suffice to explain the deep care my soul has received from your prayers and your presence. There was *No Turning Back* because of you.

Thank you, Denisse Copeland. My beautiful bride, my partner, my love, my best friend, and my number one fan. We are the true definition of a team. Thank you for your constant love and support. Thank you for always giving me space to shine brightly in the unique position God has placed me. But more so, thank you for being with me, holding me up, and honoring me every step of the way. Your love for me pours gasoline on the flame of my desire to know God's love even more.

To Jerrell, Aiden, Eli, and Samuel, my four boys. Thank you, guys, for encouraging me even as young babies who will grow into young men. I love you more than words could ever say. I pray that these words will one day bless, shape, convict, and encourage you to turn to Christ and to never turn back. Jesus loves you so much, and so do I.

To my entire Baker Books family. Thank you for believing in me and always seeing beyond what I see. I'll never forget your smiling faces cheering me on as my book *Start Where You Are* launched smack in the dead middle of a pandemic. You all walked and worked so closely with me, and it's truly been a great honor and a joy. Lindsey, Patnacia, Brianna: this is not a partnership; we truly are family. Thank you!

To my agent, Amanda Luedeke. What a joy! Here's round 2. We love you so much, and it's been a long time coming. God has truly used you to help us fuel the vision He's given to us; for that alone, I'm forever grateful for you.

To my literary therapist and friend, Jerusha Clark. Thank you for helping me hash out this book. I truly don't think I would have finished it without you. You were a huge part of every step of the way with your passionate writing support, wisdom, and counsel.

To my entire tribe of friends, family members, podcast listeners, TikTok homies, and Thursday night community group crew (you know who you are). Thank you for your relentless support. It's invaluable. Every prayer, text message, email, and word spoken over me has been used—nothing has been wasted.

Notes

Introduction

1. "Strong's G3941: paroikos," Blue Letter Bible, accessed August 4, 2021, https://www.blueletterbible.org/lexicon/g3941/niv/mgnt/0-1/.

2. "I Have Decided to Follow Jesus w/ Lyrics," YouTube video, 4:57, uploaded by Goober Sir, February 15, 2013, https://www.youtube.com/watch?v=S8jvfdDtoqY.

3. "The True Story behind the Song 'I Have Decided to Follow Jesus,'" *Renewal Journal*, November 29, 2017, https://renewaljournal.com/2017/11/29/the-true-story-behind-the-song-i-have-decided-to-follow-jesus/.

Chapter 1 From Forgetting Who You Were to Remembering Who You Are

1. Additional resources include: Neil Anderson, *Who I Am in Christ: A Devotional* (Ventura, CA: Regal, 2001); Tim Chester, *You Can Change: God's Transforming Power for Our Sinful Behavior and Negative Emotions* (Wheaton, IL: Crossway, 2010); "Identity in Christ: A Topical Survey," Desiring God, accessed September 16, 2020, https://www.desiringgod.org/topics/identity-in-christ#; "Keynote: Tim Keller—An Identity That Can Handle Either Success or Failure," YouTube video, 35:59, uploaded by New Canaan Society, June 25, 2015, https://www.youtube.com/watch?v=-N_178ASBg0.

Chapter 2 From Dirty Desires to Desiring God

1. C. S. Lewis, *Mere Christianity* (New York: HarperCollins, 2015), 205; C. S. Lewis, *The Weight of Glory: And Other Addresses* (New York: HarperCollins, 2001), 26.

2. Chester, *You Can Change*, 33.

3. John Piper, *When I Don't Desire God* (Wheaton, IL: Crossway, 2004), 16.

4. John Piper, "How to Delight in God's Word," Desiring God, March 26, 2020, https://www.desiringgod.org/articles/how-to-delight-in-gods-word.

5. Matthew Henry, *Commentary on the Whole Bible*, vol. 2 (repr., Grand Rapids: Revell, 2000), 1096.

Chapter 3 From Toxic Thinking to Transformative Truth

1. Paul David Tripp, "Are You a Functional Atheist," *Wednesday Word*, February 23, 2020, https://www.paultripp.com/wednesdays-word/posts/are-you-a-functional-atheist.

2. A. W. Tozer, *The Knowledge of the Holy* (San Francisco: Harper-Collins, 1961), 1.

3. Brother Yun and Paul Hattaway, *The Heavenly Man: The Remarkable True Story of Chinese Christian Brother Yun* (Grand Rapids: Kregel, 2002), 122.

4. Neil T. Anderson, *Victory over the Darkness: Realizing the Power of Your Identity in Christ* (Ventura, CA: Regal, 1990), 159.

Chapter 4 From Your Plan to God's Purpose

1. Credit for this phrase goes to Jamin Goggin and Kyle Strobel, *The Way of the Dragon or the Way of the Lamb: Searching for Jesus' Path of Power in a Church That Has Abandoned It* (Nashville: Nelson, 2021).

Chapter 5 From Being Spilled Empty to Being Filled with Plenty

1. Francis Chan, *The Forgotten God: Reversing Our Tragic Neglect of the Holy Spirit* (Colorado Springs: David C. Cook, 2009), 31.

2. C. Peter Wagner, *Discover Your Spiritual Gifts: The Easy-to-Use Guide That Helps You Identify and Understand Your Unique God-Given Spiritual Gifts* (Bloomington, MN: Chosen, 2017); Sam Storms, *The Beginner's Guide to Spiritual Gifts* (Bloomington, MN: Bethany House, 2013); Randy Clark and Mary Healy, *The Spiritual Gifts Handbook: Using Your Gifts to Build the Kingdom* (Bloomington, MN: Chosen, 2018).

Chapter 6 From Self-Reliance to Relying on God's Power

1. Lewis, *Mere Christianity*, 123–24.

2. Lewis, *Mere Christianity*, 122.

Chapter 7 From Slavery to Kinship

1. Cathy Free, "Abandoned as a Newborn and Called 'Dumpster Baby,' He's Now an Entrepreneur Worth Millions," *Washington Post,* December 4, 2019, https://www.washingtonpost.com/lifestyle/2019/12/04/abandoned-newborn-called-dumpster-baby-hes-now-an-entrepreneur-worth-millions/.

2. Free, "Abandoned as a Newborn."

3. Free, "Abandoned as a Newborn."

4. The Greek word translated "sons" in this passage includes both sons and daughters.

Chapter 8 From Dying Religion to Living Relationship

1. "Strong's G4657: skybalon," Blue Letter Bible, accessed August 10, 2021, https://www.blueletterbible.org/lexicon/g4657/esv/mgnt/0-1/.

Chapter 9 From Risk-Free Living to Radical Faith

1. "The Influencer Report: Engaging Gen Z and Millennials," Morning Consult, November 2019, https://morningconsult.com/influencer-report-engaging-gen-z-and-millennials/.

2. Joseph Epstein, "Think You Have a Book in You? Think Again," *New York Times*, September 28, 2002, https://www.nytimes.com/2002/09/28/opinion/think-you-have-a-book-in-you-think-again.html.

3. Richard Wurmbrand, *Tortured for Christ*, Kindle ed. (Bartlesville, OK: Living Sacrifice Book Co., 2010), Kindle loc. 45–50.

4. Wurmbrand, *Tortured for Christ*, loc. 57–58, 64.

5. Wurmbrand, *Tortured for Christ*, loc. 71, 73.

6. Wurmbrand, *Tortured for Christ*, loc. 105–12.

7. Wurmbrand, *Tortured for Christ*, loc. 105–12.

8. Wurmbrand, *Tortured for Christ*, loc. 535–36.

9. Dictionary.com, s.v. "tourist," accessed December 10, 2020, https://www.dictionary.com/browse/tourist?s=t.

10. Dictionary.com, s.v. "sojourn," accessed December 11, 2020, https://www.dictionary.com/browse/sojourn#.

11. Read all about it in Eugene Peterson, *A Long Obedience in the Same Direction: Discipleship in an Instant Society*, commemorative ed. (Wheaton: InterVarsity, 2019).

12. Jan Hus, "Vyklad Viry," as quoted in Thomas A. Fudge, *Jan Hus: Religious Reform and Social Revolution in Bohemia* (London: I.B. Tauris, 2017), 233.

Afterthought

1. John Bunyan, *Pilgrim's Progress*, updated ed. (Abbotsford, WI: Aneko Press, 2014), 227.

2. Bunyan, *Pilgrim's Progress*, 228.

3. Jonathan Edwards, "The Christian Pilgrim (or The True Christian's Life a Journey Toward Heaven)," sermon preached in Boston, September 1733, Sermon Index, accessed December 14, 2020, https://www.sermonindex.net/modules/articles/index.php?view=article&aid=3416.

Rashawn Copeland is the author of *Start Where You Are* and the founder of I'm So Blessed Daily and Without Walls Ministries. Founder of the largest Christian Facebook network, which reaches millions daily, he is also the host of the *Scriptures and Stories* podcast on the Converge Podcast Network. He has served alongside notable brands such as Life Church (YouVersion), the Manny Pacquiao Foundation, the Museum of the Bible, Pureflix, and many others. A graduate of the University of Central Oklahoma, he is currently earning his MDiv at Liberty University and lives in Oklahoma City with his wife, Denisse, and their four children.

CONNECT WITH
RASHAWN

Jesus was always passionate about people. His greatest ability was His availability. Rashawn is excited to get to know you. He'd love to chat with you! If you want to speak with him, reach out to Rashawn@blessedmedia.co.

You can also reach out to him on

 **@hypesir**    **@hypesir7**

Here's his phone number if you'd like to give him a call:
(469) 877-8408

Rashawn is open to visiting your college, conference, church, or audience to host, keynote, or share a message. Rashawn is a minister who writes and a writer who speaks. He has a unique perspective, and he's a passionate storyteller. If you are interested in having Rashawn visit your event, contact Rashawn@blessedmedia.co.

I'M SO BLESSED DAILY

Looking for your daily dose of good news?
Check out I'm So Blessed Daily for inspiration
and blessing every day!

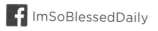 ImSoBlessedDaily

 imsoblesseddailyofficial

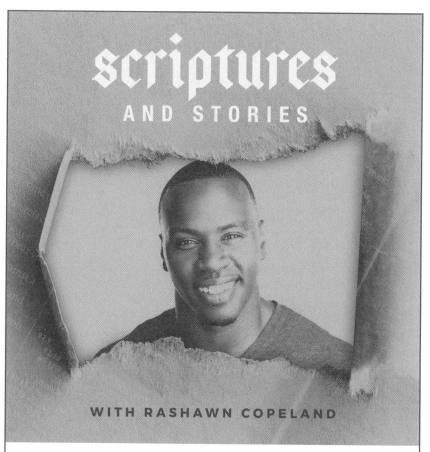

scriptures
AND STORIES

WITH RASHAWN COPELAND

Scriptures and Stories is a podcast all about sharing ordinary stories from fantastic guests. You will hear their favorite Scriptures and their stories of God's hand in their life.

Join Rashawn Copeland on this journey to fall in love with God's Word through the stories of God's people.

TUNE IN WHEREVER YOU LISTEN TO PODCASTS.

NO MATTER WHERE YOU ARE,

that's exactly where God promises to meet you.

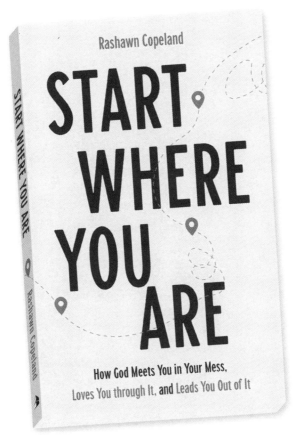

Sharing his own story of spiritual drifting, popular online pastor Rashawn Copeland encourages you to accept yourself as a glorious work in progress, a beloved child in whom God delights, a person on the brink of revival. Anchoring everything in Scripture, he shows you how to start your walk with God *now*, even in the midst of your mess.

BakerBooks
a division of Baker Publishing Group
www.BakerBooks.com

Available wherever books and ebooks are sold.